UNDER A CLOUD OF SAILS

UNDER A CLOUD OF SAILS

MEMOIRS OF A FREE SPIRIT

WINSTON WILLIAMS

BONITA SPRINGS, FL

Copyright © 2020 by Winston Williams

All rights reserved.

Published in the United States by O'Leary Publishing

All rights reserved. No part of this publication may be reproduced, distributed, or transmitted in any form or by any means, including photocopying, recording, or other electronic or mechanical methods, without the prior written permission of the publisher, except in the case of brief quotations embodied in critical reviews and certain other noncommercial uses permitted by copyright law. For permission requests, write to the publisher, addressed "Attention: Permissions Coordinator," at the address below.

The views, information, or opinions expressed in this book are solely those of the authors involved and do not necessarily represent those of O'Leary Publishing, LLC.

Any references to historical events, real people, or places are written from the author's best recollection of past events.

ISBN: 978-1-68454-115-7 (Paperback)
ISBN: 978-1-7341589-7-7 (eBook)
Library of Congress Control Number: 2019917630

Back cover image by Winston Williams
Book design by Jessica Angerstein
Edited by Heather Davis Desrocher
Illustration by James P. Brown

Printed in the United States of America
First printing edition 2020

O'Leary Publishing
28089 Vanderbilt Drive Suite 202
Bonita Springs, FL 34134
www.olearypublishing.com

Dedicated to my brother Donnie and to my four children Lilli, Ricky, Phil, and Caroline.

CONTENTS

Preface..ix

Part I

Chapter 1: The Beginning................................... 1
Chapter 2: The Preparation 13
Chapter 3: Under A Cloud Of Sails 23
Chapter 4: Odyssey...33
Chapter 5: Pitcairn And Beyond..........................43
Chapter 6: Tahiti And The Pacific........................51
Chapter 7: New Guinea And The Far East 63
Chapter 8: The Indian Ocean To Africa................73
Chapter 9: Homeward Bound 85
Chapter 10: In Limbo..93
Chapter 11: Utopian Interlude............................97
Chapter 12: First Command 109
Chapter 13: Pearl Diving On Takaroa 123

Part II

Chapter 14: Settling Down............................... 135
Chapter 15: The Avenue Of Addiction................ 145
Chapter 16: Returning Home 157

Chapter 17: The 23 Steps 169
Chapter 18: Revival. 179
Chapter 19: Cape Cod 185
Chapter 20: The Reunion 195

Part III
Chapter 21: Return To The Cape. 207
Chapter 22: Down To The Sea Again 219
Chapter 23: On The Bridge Deck 231
Chapter 24: Chesapeake Country. 241
Chapter 25: Florida. 251
Chapter 26: Naples 257
Chapter 27: California Odyssey 269
Chapter 28: Resettlement. 277
Chapter 29: I'm Done 287
Chapter 30: A Look Back 297

Epilogue 303
Glossary 305
Photobook 309
Acknowledgments. 329
About the Author. 331

PREFACE

RECENTLY I was sitting on the beach in La Jolla, California, playing in the sand with 5-year-old Olivia, one of my 12 grandchildren. We were busy building castles using her little plastic shovels and buckets. Suddenly she looked up in the sky and exclaimed, "Look, Grandpa! See them fly?" I looked up and saw a flock of gulls flying overhead. Then she looked at me and said, "Let's sing happy birthday to the seagulls!" So, like any self-respecting grandfather, I joined her, and we sang happy birthday as they flew off into the distance.

Later while driving back to Orange County where I was living, I thought about that moment. The saying ". . . out of the mouth of babes" kept running through my mind. Olivia's outburst was priceless. It showed the free-spiritedness and wonder for the world that every child has - two personality traits that I have always been blessed to have and which have had a great influence in my life, steering it to many strange and adventurous situations and places. A few days later I was sharing with a close friend what had happened and my reaction. "Why don't you write a book Win," she said. "You've led a remarkable life."

I thought about it and warmed to the idea. Looking back on my life I realized I had nearly done it all. I was a chronic sailor and adventurer, having circled the world in a tall ship. I was movie star Sterling Hayden's 1st mate on his schooner in the South Seas and sailed my own schooner on a 4,000-mile odyssey to Tahiti. Later in life, I was everything from a corporate executive, published author and commercial boat captain, to a limo driver, car rental employee, bus driver, boatyard worker, and an alcoholism counselor. Because of this diverse life, many of my friends have urged me to write a book of memoirs.

I have finally listened to them. Hopefully, these chapters will bring readers vicariously through this adventurous, sometimes complicated life.

PART I

CHAPTER ONE

THE BEGINNING

In the year 1935, the average cost of a new home was $3,450. Gas cost 10 cents a gallon, new cars could be bought for $625, and Babe Ruth hit his 714th and final home run. There was also an early morning thunderstorm over the Gramercy Park Hospital on 23rd Street in Manhattan, at the moment I was born on July 13th of that year.

When I was six months old my Mom, Dad and older brother Donnie moved to Bernardsville, New Jersey, a town in the country

30 miles west of Manhattan. They rented a home to stay in until they found a property to purchase where they could build a permanent home.

My father, Donald Rowe Williams, had graduated from Yale University eight years previously and was now working as an executive for the Union News Company, a distributing corporation that his father had co-founded. For a long time, Dad would make the one-hour commute to his office in Rockefeller Center. To get there he rode the Lackawanna Railroad train which ran through the Morristown station 10 miles away. His commute to Hoboken took an hour, after which he caught the ferry across the Hudson River to lower Manhattan.

Elizabeth Williams, my mother, was born in Philadelphia. When she was older, her father, because of health reasons, moved the family to Pasadena, California to continue his business affairs and she went to an exclusive private school where she excelled as a student. Later in her early teens, the family moved back to the East Coast. As an adult, she got her first, and what would be the only, job of her life as an employee at a Manhattan retail store. This eventually led to meeting Dad. At the time, she was renting an apartment on the East side with a friend. As things worked out Dad happened to be dating this roommate of hers and, inevitably, met Mom. After one look, he realized he had been dating the wrong woman. Dropping the roommate, he began dating Mom, and that was that. Just a year later on February 1st, 1930, they were married.

I was too young to remember those days in Bernardsville. My earliest memories go back to my life in our newly built home at Mendham just 15 miles away. In 1938 my parents had found some beautiful property halfway between the town of Morristown and the small village of Mendham. Its 15 acres lay in the country on a picturesque hillside looking out over a valley and a small stream. In the back of the house was a field of small cedar trees with golden, waist-high grass, surrounded by a deciduous forest and hedgerows of dogwood. The house was built on the downhill side of this field overlooking the valley below. A winding driveway led up the hill from Leddell Road, a single lane dirt road which was never paved for the entire 15 years we lived there. From our home, not one other house could be seen.

Because our house was built on a hillside, its front side had three stories and the backside had only two. The front and back doors were Dutch doors, the kind that had halves so the upper parts could be opened in the spring and summer. Being a large house, it had six bedrooms, four on the top floor and a master bedroom and guest room downstairs. The stairs had banisters which, to the disapproval of our parents, Donnie and I often slid down on. Inviting fireplaces were located in the living room and dining room on the ground floor.

When I was five or six, our parents hired a live-in cook. She was an African-American woman who must have weighed at least 250 pounds, and her name was Rose. She was kind and gentle and a wonderful cook. I clearly remember the times when Mom and Dad went out to cocktail and dinner parties. They would have to walk through the kitchen to get to the garage. As Rose was cooking on the old Aga stove, she'd look up as they came through—Dad dressed in grey flannels, blazer and tie and Mom in an evening dress. Rose would exclaim, "My word, Mr. and Mrs. Williams. You two look like the bride and groom!" And after they left, Rose would feed Donnie and me at the kitchen table. Often we'd misbehave, and she would scold us by saying, "What are you two doing? You think you was in the crazy house!" Rose stayed with us for many years, and we all loved her. We also had a nurse named Francis who came in days and looked after me in my childhood years.

In 1940, at the brink of World War II, my brother and I attended the Peck School. We would be picked up by the Peck school bus, which was an Oldsmobile station wagon. To meet the bus, the two of us would walk a quarter of a mile down our driveway and along Leddell Road and, finally, to the mailboxes on Tempe Wick Road where we would wait.

Shortly after, Dad would start his drive to the Lackawanna Railroad Station in Morristown, catch the train to Hoboken and, eventually, arrive at his Manhattan office at the Union News Company before 9:00. In the evenings when Dad returned home from work, he and mother would relax in the library and drink a couple of Manhattans before dinner. Our television, a new medium which would eventually replace the radio, was tuned in to the news with Edward R. Murrow. It was a peaceful time for Donnie and me, who would sit on the rug and wrestle with Portley, our Old English Sheepdog, while Mom and Dad sipped their drinks. I remember these moments in the library as being some of the more intimate times we spent together as a family.

We all loved Portley, who was a big, long-haired, affectionate dog and the perfect pet. He was a breed of sheepdog which were used to herd sheep on the moors of England and Scotland. Although Portley had never seen sheep, Dad was always curious about what he would do if he was surrounded by a herd of them. Just by chance, our neighbors, the Brunets, had a pasture with a dozen sheep. One day we took Portley over and let him loose. Amazingly, despite being the first time he had ever seen sheep, he had them crowded in a knot in five minutes flat as he raced around them in increasingly tight circles. Dad never had to wonder about Portley's abilities again.

There were some moments which, in themselves, didn't seem significant but turned out to be harbingers of things to come. One moment was when I was just nine-years-old. I remember lying on my back in the tall golden field grass and looking up at the sky. Fascinated with the thunderheads and white puffy clouds, I experienced a wonder, curiosity, and enthusiasm for what I saw. This same enthusiasm and curiosity would, in later years, have a significant influence on my life.

At about the same age, I remember hearing the song of the Wood thrush in the early summer evenings, as Mom and Dad would have their cocktails out on the terrace in the back of the house. During this serene family time together, the thrushes in the nearby woods would sing their flute-like songs. To this day I have never heard more beautiful music than these warbling thrush songs. It was the start of a lifelong interest in birds and birdwatching, an activity which became even more appealing when Donnie took me down to the valley field early one morning. There he pointed out a spectacular Chestnut-sided Warbler whose colors radiated in the sun. Since that time so long ago, I have continued to count and enjoy all the different species of birds I have seen to the point that recently my "life list" topped 400.

Then there were the moments when I had essays to write as a seventh-grader at Peck School. I always earned good grades because I discovered I loved to write. The fact that I had a creative side was not a surprise. I had inherited it from Mom whose creativity showed in her gardens. In our backyard, she had grown the most beautiful, well laid out flower garden in the area. In later years Mom's gardens would attract tours of flower lovers and, at one time, she was the President of the local garden club.

Perhaps the most influential moment happened in 1946 when I was 11 years old. One late afternoon Dad arrived home from work and announced to Mom that he had resigned his vice president's job and was to start as a history teacher at St. Bernard's School in nearby Gladstone. Mom had a fit. I suppose any wife would have reacted the same way because Dad's five-figure salary as a senior executive would shrink to $7,000 a year. He was in his early 40's and Mom felt he was giving up a great career as a corporate executive. None of us knew then that eventually, Dad would become headmaster of St. Bernard's and, later on, a dean of admissions at Yale University. This decision of his had a great effect on me. Dad's strong desire to follow his passions, and do what he really wanted to do in life, influenced me years later to do the same thing. "Follow your bliss," as the philosopher Joseph Campbell once said, was to be my theme in life, just as it had been Dad's.

Sometimes things happen which suddenly change your life, leading it in a new direction. I was 11 years old at the time and in my room, supposedly taking my compulsory afternoon nap. There happened to be a pile of recent National Geographic magazines which Dad had stored in my closet. I took one out and began reading it. Flipping through the pages I came to an article that caught my attention. It was about a couple who had sailed around the world three times aboard a 100-foot Dutch pilot schooner called *Yankee*, taking with them an amateur crew of 20. Their names were Irving and Electa Johnson. The voyages lasted a year and a half, and they visited places like Pitcairn Island, Tahiti, New Guinea, Bangkok, and Capetown. Johnson, a seasoned sailor, and navigator, filmed the voyages and then on his return to the States edited the footage and went on lecture tours across the country before the next world trip set sail. There was a new crew picked for each voyage and together they shared the expenses.

Fascinated, I read the article twice and intently studied photographs of the Pitcairners, descendants of the *Bounty* mutineers in 1789, Tahiti and its incomparable beauty, South Africa and the voyage up the South Atlantic in the trade winds. There were also photos of the crew members themselves. Their average age was 20, and there were three women in the crew.

The article excited me. Just like most 11-year-old boys who want to be a fireman or policeman when they grow up, I knew I wanted to sail on this *Yankee*. As a matter of fact, I was so enthused, I sat down and wrote a letter to the Johnsons. Surprisingly, a month later they answered, saying I was a little young to be a crew member but, perhaps, they could get together with me later when I was college age. From that moment on, going on the *Yankee* became an obsession. I would think of little else in the coming years.

Twelve months later, at the age of 12, I began a long six-year stint at the Groton School, an exclusive boarding school in Massachusetts, whose most famous graduate was former President Franklin Delano Roosevelt. My brother Donnie had already been at Groton for four years, and Dad had been a graduate way back in 1923. Groton was a strict Episcopalian church school modeled after the private school system in England. Besides the normal courses found at high schools, Groton also offered Latin and French classes. The strictness of the school was reflected in the way we had to dress and behave. Blue blazers and ties were compulsory and the no-nonsense rules during study halls and in the dormitories at night were rigorously enforced. We were required to attend church services before classes each morning and were only allowed to eat out at the town restaurants when our parents visited.

During my time at Groton, I excelled in sports. I was one of the youngest to ever make the varsity hockey team, I played right field for the baseball varsity and, years later, I was voted onto the all-time Groton soccer team. I loved sports and was a natural athlete. Other than creative writing, where I had natural abilities, I wasn't a gifted student. I was a scholastic disaster. However, I managed to graduate from school by the skin of my teeth.

Except for athletics, I never felt entirely comfortable or fully a part of school life for the six years I spent at Groton for several reasons. The first was my obsession with going around the world on the *Yankee*. It had become a priority and was my focus in life. I was a dreamer and this was my dream. It seldom occurred to me that Irving Johnson might not make future world voyages or that I wouldn't be accepted as a crew member. It was only during my graduating year that I learned there would be a final seventh world cruise in 1956.

The second reason was more deep-seated. It started with my grandfather, the co-founder of the Union News Company, whom I had never met. At an early age, I learned of his compassion and interest in those less fortunate than him. The janitor of his building was as important to him as his other employees. Dad had inherited that trait and it, in turn, had been transferred to me. Many of my friends outside of Groton were high school students and had parents who were carpenters or construction workers.

This inherent urge to identify with the common man made it uncomfortable for me to be surrounded by students in a school that was for the privileged. This is not to say I didn't like my classmates. There were a few who I became close to. It wasn't a question of disliking or being disapproving of the elite. Instead, it was an inherent urge I had to identify with everyone, not just the well-to-do. Be that as it may, this prevented me from getting close to many of my schoolmates. The fact was that in future years I would lose touch with many of them, and I went to few reunions.

Then there was a great emphasis on what Groton thought of as "success." Today many of my classmates have had careers as CEOs, businessmen, politicians, and lawyers. Money making and prominence in one's field was given great importance. But I was not as fired up about that as the school wanted me to be. I had different priorities. The simple fact was I would have preferred to be listening to the song of the Wood thrush or appreciating a moon path on the water more than concentrating on Latin classes and the importance of becoming a successful banker earning a six-figure salary.

Finally, I had trouble with the religious and social views of the school. Like all religions, the Episcopal Church had certain ways of doing things and strict doctrines. The truth was I didn't like someone telling me what to believe. I had my own beliefs. I was a rebel. I suppose it was this part of me that caused my parents, especially Mom, to disapprove and worry. Mom was strict and unswerving in her life. As far as she was concerned, one associated with the *right* people practiced a respectable profession and followed the rules set by social standards. This difference between us caused a lot of friction which, unfortunately, would last until the day she died at the age of 97. In later years, I was to realize her negative reactions were a product of her generation and that I could have done more to smooth out our relationship.

I don't mean in any way to attack Groton as an institution. To this day it is unquestionably one of the finest schools in the country. My Dad and brother Donnie loved the school. It was just that I was on a different wavelength.

Graduation day finally came in 1953. I had applied for entrance to Yale but, despite the fact that my father went there and that my brother was currently a student, my marks were too low and I was denied admittance. My second application to Trinity College in Hartford, however, was accepted, and I started making plans for my freshman year in the fall.

But uppermost in my mind was sailing on *Yankee* whose seventh world cruise in the fall of 1956 had been confirmed.

CHAPTER 2

THE PREPARATION

'M NOT sure when Mom and Dad decided to summer on Nantucket Island, Massachusetts. Dad was still with the Union News Company and had three weeks' vacation a year. So at some point my parents chose to try a summer in Nantucket and see if they liked it there. It seemed like a good place to get away from it all for a couple of weeks and friends had highly recommended it.

Our first summer was in 1942 when I was seven years old. It was love at first sight for all of us, and in 1946 Mom and Dad purchased a three-bedroom vacation home on North Liberty Street just outside of town. We were to be owners of that house for the next 60 years.

At that time Nantucket was a wonderful, quiet and charming place that boasted 54 miles of white beaches, historic homes and a slow pace of life. The island lay 30 miles offshore from Cape Cod, attracting tourists and summer residents from May through September. The island had an interesting history, at one time being a major whaling port of the world despite its small size of 30,000 acres. Stately, historic homes of whaling ship owners, who lived there in the 1840's, stood on each side of the cobblestones of upper Main Street and in the shade of tall elm trees. On lower Main Street, the bank, insurance office, two pharmacies and a mom-and-pop newspaper store quietly did business. It was unspoken that the half dozen benches on each side of the street were reserved for the older Nantucket natives, although this rule was often broken by tourists.

Outside of town there were undulating moors which turned red in the fall and were crisscrossed by sand roads winding to and fro. And, of course, the endless beaches around the island overlooking Nantucket Sound to the north, and the Atlantic Ocean to the south, offered countless places to swim.

It was here on Nantucket that I finally became aware of my intense love for the sea. When I was 12, I remember riding my bike ten miles to Tom Nevers Head, a bluff which rose from the beach below and looked out over the Atlantic Ocean beyond.

Here, I spent hours sitting at its edge studying the ocean and wondering what lay beyond the horizon. My mind swam with dreams and fantasies of voyages to faraway places, imagining the possibility of my seeing those places if I ever got on one of the *Yankee's* world cruises.

My love for the sea became even more apparent when my parents joined the Nantucket Yacht Club and arranged for me to take some sailing lessons. An instructor named Toppy Lindsay took me out in a 12-foot Beetlecat. Before we got back to the dock it was obvious to him that I had an above average instinct as a sailor. By my third lesson I soloed. I remember the thrill of being alone and able to sail any direction I wanted. It seemed like I naturally knew what to do and I had the confidence to do it.

The next summer, a year later, Dad bought me a brand new Beetlecat. I called it *Whirlaway* after the famous Kentucky Derby horse. Right away I took up competition with the 20 other Beetlecats. The fleet was known as the Rainbow Fleet because of the different brightly colored sails each beetle had. Races were organized by the Nantucket Yacht Club and were scheduled every Tuesday and Thursday afternoon during the months of July and August. Pennants were awarded to those who came in first, second or third in the individual races. Engraved cups were given at the end of each month to the overall month winner and a championship trophy for the entire summer.

Immediately I started winning races or placing second or third in most of them. At the end of that summer I had pennants hanging from my bedroom wall with a trophy on my bureau. In succeeding summers I continued to win frequently and was considered one of the top sailors in the fleet.

Later in my teens I had other sailing opportunities on bigger boats and on a few yachts. The most interesting of these was the 60-foot brigantine *Black Pearl*, a beautiful clipper-bowed vessel owned and built in Rhode Island by the father of a Groton friend of mine, Wheaton Vaughn. *Black Pearl* had four yards on her foremast and a gaff-rigged mainsail making her look like a small version of a clipper ship under sail. Cruising to Block Island and around Narragansett Bay, I "learned the ropes" from Wheaton and his father and had my first bona fide experience on a square-rigged sailing vessel.

This was significant in light of the fact that Irving and Electa Johnson had sold their schooner, which they had sailed three times around the world, and purchased a new *Yankee* just after World War II whose rig was a brigantine. She had been built in 1914 as a German North Sea pilot boat, the last sailing pilot boat the Germans used before they changed to power-driven vessels. The Johnsons planned to do a fifth and sixth world cruise and were considering a seventh and final one in 1956 with their new 96-foot *Yankee*. This was the trip I would go on if I was accepted as a crew member. This possibility would make my time on the *Black Pearl*, as brief as it was, valuable square-rig experience, and it would look good on my resume.

My summers on Nantucket were not the only times when my dream of sailing on *Yankee* was nourished. At school I spent hours of reading in the library, my favorite place at Groton, feeding my dream even more. I poured over countless books on the history of the Age of Sail and stories of the old square-riggers and clipper ships. I read Villiers, Underhill and the prose of John Masefield. I also developed an interest in some of the places that the *Yankee* would visit, particularly Polynesia and the islands of Tahiti, the Tuamotu atolls and the Marquesas. *Mutiny on the Bounty* by Charles Nordoff and James Norman Hall got me interested in Pitcairn Island, the place where the mutineers had fled and hid from the British authorities. To this day their descendants live there, and the island had been part of the Johnsons' itinerary on every trip they had made.

In my senior year at Groton, the Johnsons had nearly completed their sixth cruise around the world. One day I learned they were definitely planning a seventh cruise starting in May of 1956. With a great deal of excitement, I wrote a letter to them saying I was as interested as ever in going.

Of course, my life, from the time I was a Groton student until I was a freshman at Trinity, was filled with other things besides my *Yankee* dream. After I turned 16, I earned my driver's license, a big event for any teenager. I started dating and going to the usual society dances in Manhattan which were held at the Biltmore, the Waldorf-Astoria and other high class hotels. Night beach parties on Nantucket during the summers introduced me to alcohol, and

I discovered that I loved to drink, something that would have a great effect on my life in later years.

I graduated from Groton in 1954 when I was 18. As a graduation gift, Dad bought me a used 1952 Chevrolet for $800. It was green, had four doors and boasted "Power Glide," Chevy's first automatic transmission. I drove it to Trinity college that fall to start my freshman year. The next spring, two of my college roommates and I drove my car down to Fort Lauderdale, Florida for "spring break" where we would sleep on the beach and in the backroom of a store owned by a kind businessman.

As at Groton, my freshman year at Trinity proved me to be a mediocre student. Again, it wasn't that I didn't have the ability so much as a lack of focus on studying. Drinking, dating and performing "donuts" with my car on snow-covered college parking lots were priorities. The one course I did excel in was creative writing, and later the college's magazine *The Trinity Review* would publish an article I wrote. It was to be my first publication as a writer.

And, of course, no matter what I was doing, there was my dream of sailing on *Yankee* lurking just below the surface.

The telephone call came in the spring of my freshman year while I was attending a creative writing class. Leaving the classroom and following the student who had given me the note, I went into a nearby office where someone was holding a telephone receiver. The voice that said "hello" was Irving Johnson's. He asked me if I could drive the 30 miles to Longmeadow that afternoon

THE PREPARATION

where he could interview me in his brother's home. I was so excited that I was actually talking to him, I didn't remember saying "yes."

I didn't go back to the creative writing class. Instead, I went outside and walked up and down the quadrangle, fully absorbed with what had just happened. The culmination of a dream that had started years ago when I was 12 seemed suddenly to be coming true. I felt spaced out, not quite believing it was happening.

Hours later I found myself driving up Route 91 to Longmeadow, my excitement growing with each mile. I thought of the times years before when I was at Tom Nevers Head on Nantucket, looking out over the sea and wondering what lay beyond the horizon. The memories of my first solo trip on the Beetlecat, the races in *Whirlaway* and my cruise on the *Black Pearl* all came back to me in a rush. And I recalled the day way back when I was 12, picking up that issue of National Geographic and reading one of Johnson's articles—a day when a childhood dream was born - one I had tenuously hung on to.

So absorbed in thought, I nearly missed the Longmeadow exit. Following the directions given to me, I took the off-ramp, drove into a residential area and finally found their home. As I walked up the path to the front door, my heart was racing. It was Irving Johnson himself who opened the door and invited me in.

The interview lasted two hours. During the whole time, Electa, or Exy as everyone called her, sat quietly nearby knitting a sweater as Irving went into a long monologue about the world cruises.

Afterwards, he asked me some questions but not nearly as many as I had expected. Very few were about my sailing experiences which qualified me as a candidate. Most of his questions centered around my expectations. Would I be able to sleep in a 6-foot bunk for 18 months? How did I feel about being freezing cold in an Atlantic gale in the middle of the night? Occasionally, Exy would ask a question, too. I realized they were more interested in my character than my sailing experience. One thing was clear. They saw my enthusiasm and determination to sail on *Yankee* and recalled the letter I had written to them as a 12-year-old.

Near the end of the interview, Johnson described what they did during the summers prior to the world cruises. For the next two summers, he said, they would be taking different groups of girl scout mariners for one week cruises along the New England coast as they had always done. And then he took me completely by surprise with his next question.

"Would you like to sail with us for the next two summers as an apprentice for the 3rd mate position on the world cruise?"

"Yes!!" I exclaimed, practically jumping out of my chair.

My dream was coming true!

One final hurdle remained. I needed consent from my parents. On a weekend shortly after the interview, I drove home to New Jersey to break the news. They weren't unaware of my dream. I had mentioned it numerous times since its beginning when I was 12, but I don't believe they took it too seriously. Or if they had, they dismissed it as one of those childhood fantasies which would disappear as I grew older.

With an admittedly manipulative move, I chose to tell them Saturday evening during cocktails, the family's peaceful "together" time. They listened quietly as they sipped their Manhattans and the spring thrushes sang in the backwoods. When I finished, there was silence. Then Mother began to voice her objections. She feared that after the cruise was over, I would never go back to college and graduate. Dad agreed. I argued that they had nothing to fear and I would definitely go back to Trinity when I returned. Besides, I added, the cruise would be in itself a unique education where I would have a chance to see the different cultures of the world and how people lived. After arguing back and forth for a while, they realized how determined I was to go and that I had already committed myself to the Johnsons.

In the end they reluctantly agreed, although Mother, more than Dad, never bothered to hide her reluctance to let me go. In her mind, I should have been following the path my brother Donnie was taking. That was to finish college, go to law school and become a lawyer or a pursuit similar to that. I knew she felt I would never return to college.

Although I was excited by their consent, I drove back to Trinity the next day nurturing a resentment of Mother's obvious disapproval. It was years later when I would realize that she and Dad had been willing to come up with $5000 required by each crew member to share in the expenses of the cruise. In addition,

I would finally appreciate that, even though they disapproved of my going, they backed down and let me do what I wanted. This was a true gift from them.

When I returned to Trinity, it was impossible to keep my mind off the impending summer aboard *Yankee*. I couldn't believe that in just two months I'd be sailing with the Johnsons along the coast of New England in preparation for the seventh world cruise two years later on November 4th, 1956. Indeed, it was almost a miracle that I passed my spring courses and became a sophomore for the following fall semester.

CHAPTER 3

UNDER A CLOUD OF SAILS

I T WAS August and we were racing down Narragansett Bay in Rhode Island. The fresh northwest wind off our starboard quarter whipped up lines of white caps, and puffy, cumulus clouds overhead accentuated the blue sky. *Yankee* was on a rampage. Under all sail with topgallant, foretopsail and foresail billowing with wind, her bow pushed white water like a plow pushes snow, and her stern left a foamy path behind. We were making 12 knots, which was *Yankee's* maximum hull speed, and we must have made a beautiful sight. A writer in the last century once wrote that one of the most beautiful things in the world was a square-rigged vessel under full sail. This must have been evident to the three fishermen on board an incoming dragger. As they passed, they threw their hats in the air in salute and waved their arms enthusiastically.

I had joined the Johnsons two months earlier after finishing my spring term at college. Since then we had been sailing up and down the New England coast, picking up different groups of Girl Scout mariners. We had been to: Fisher's Island; Mystic and Block Island, along the Connecticut coast; sailed to Newport, Rhode Island; and had visited: Nantucket, Cuttyhunk and Marion in Massachusetts. We even sailed north to Lunenburg, Nova Scotia. The crew consisted of: Ed Crosby from Osterville, Cape Cod; Robert Johnson, the 19-year-old son of the Johnsons; John Blanchard, the acting 1st mate; Ken Viard, the cook; and myself. And then, of course, there was "Skipper," as Irving liked to be called, and Exy.

On the average, there were around 15 Girl Scout mariners in a group. Each group sailed with us for a week and then was replaced by a new one. The girls weren't allowed to go aloft, so most of the sail handling was left to the six of us. Because of this, we had to hustle and work hard to handle things which normally needed twice as many hands. The girls would help by hauling the halyards on deck. It required 10 hands or more to set the mainsail, 5 on the main halyard and 5 on the peak halyard. But anything aloft could only be done by the regular crew members. We'd climb up and lay out on the footropes of the yards 80 feet above the deck to set or furl the square sails. Often, the man next to me would be Skipper himself, who had given the wheel to Exy, and then he would run up the ratlines with us.

The summer turned out to be a crash course on seamanship and sailing. And I loved it. I learned to splice, serve and seize lines. I memorized where each of the more than 30 lines were located so I could find them, even in the dark. I was introduced to sewing patches on sails, whipping lines and endless painting and varnishing.

And because the *Yankee* had no fathometer, a type of echo-sounder, the old art of throwing the lead line was practiced. This was my favorite job. A 5-pound lead was tied onto a long clothesline which had marks identifying fathoms (a fathom equaled 6 feet). Every mark was either a piece of leather, a seizing or a piece of cloth each 6 feet apart. I'd stand on a special step by the bow and toss the lead ahead into the water. As it sunk to the bottom, I'd take up the slack in the line as the ship caught up to it. Then I would note which mark was nearest to the surface of the water and shout out the depth to Skipper aft, "By the mark three!" I would yell, indicating the depth was 3 fathoms, or 18 feet; or "a quarter less four!" meaning about 22 feet.

The *Yankee* didn't have the navigational technology of today. For instance, there wasn't a single winch on board. Halyards were "sweated up" by hand – in some cases by many hands. GPS had not even been heard of, and we had no Loran or radar. To find our coastal positions, we used our hands, lining up the compass with any point on shore to get bearings. Offshore navigation was done by sextant and H.O.214 tables. In other words, we sailed the ship. With today's technology, it's the opposite. The ship tends to sail the crew.

Yankee had two diesel engines which Skipper ran sparingly. Whenever possible, he used any or all 7700 square feet of sail for maneuvering up to or away from anchorages and docks, if wind direction allowed it. This could make for some exciting and dramatic moments because we were so shorthanded and sometimes needed to be in two places at once. Skipper was a show-off and he loved to impress others with his engineless maneuvering.

I remember sometime that July when we were approaching Block Island, a southwest wind was on our starboard quarter, and we were under full sail. As we came near the entrance of Great Salt Pond, we realized that the New York Yacht Club fleet was anchored there. Without hesitation, Skipper boldly slipped through the middle of the entire fleet, shouting orders to us as we frantically shortened sail. Then, with the mainsail sheeted in and foretopsail set, he spun the *Yankee* around into the wind so that the latter sail came back and acted as a brake while the anchor was let go. It was a performance which the New York Yacht Club obviously admired, and some of its blue-blazered owners, to Skipper's satisfaction, even blew their horns. Irving Johnson was well qualified to do such things.

In 1929, as a 19-year-old, he had sailed around Cape Horn aboard one of the few remaining bona fide grain ships, the 4-masted barque *Peking*. Prior to World War II, he and Exy had taken the schooner *Yankee* around the world three times. When the war came, he served as a lieutenant commander in the Navy and commanded a 200-foot survey vessel. Just after the war he purchased the new *Yankee* which, at the time, was in Brixham, England, where she was being kept as a prize of war by the British. Owned and built by the Germans in 1914, she had been used as a pilot boat in the North Sea. Later, the British had captured her during World War II and taken her to England. When the war was over, Sterling Hayden, the movie actor who had been 1st mate on the Johnsons' 1st world cruise, saw the vessel and told Irving about it. Skipper travelled to Brixham and promptly bought her, naming her *Yankee*. Then he sailed her to the States and prepared for the 4th world cruise. One of the things he did was change her rig from schooner to brigantine. His reasoning was that all the world cruises went through the trade wind belts. He knew the most efficient rig for sailing before the wind was square-rig.

So it was a prize of war I was sailing on. She was 96 feet long and had a large main cabin lined by 23 bunks with Skipper and Exy's cabin aft. A galley was located forward with a large dining table in the main cabin. Because the girls used the main cabin's bunks, Ed and I slept in the forepeak. This was a small space forward accessible by a hatch and stepladder where spare lines, sails and other gear were stowed. We literally slept on a storm trysail from June to September.

The summer ended before I knew it. As I was leaving, skipper reassured me that he expected me to return next summer and that I was to be 3rd mate on the world cruise which would follow on November 4, 1956. I returned home to spend a short time with Mom and Dad and then headed back to Trinity for the fall semester. I was so preoccupied, however, by the impending *Yankee* trip that it was very difficult to make the transition back to being a student.

Despite the trouble I had focusing on college life, my sophomore year passed surprisingly quickly. Winter and spring terms came and went. And then I found myself sailing on *Yankee* for my second summer. Ed and I slept in the forepeak again. There was a different group of Girl Scout mariners each week like the previous year, and I continued to be molded into a better sailor. And I had more opportunities to practice navigation, becoming proficient with the sextant and working out lines of position on the chart using the H.O. 214 tables.

Our itinerary was much the same except that we sailed to Nantucket a few more times than the year before. My 21st birthday was during one of these visits. I was excused from the ship for 24 hours and was able to celebrate with my parents at the house on North Liberty Street. During dinner, my godfather Gilman Low, who for a long time had been close friends with Mom and

Dad, presented me with a bottle of old wine. He had saved it for 20 years just so that he could give it to me on my 21st birthday. We celebrated late into the night, and it was the first time I got drunk in front of my parents. I woke up in the morning with a bad hangover, but I didn't give it any thought because I had gotten drunk several times before with my roommates at college, and it wasn't a big deal. Also, I had gone out with Ed to a few bars while we were in port. In my mind, it was all quite normal.

Later in August we returned to Nantucket, and I stayed overnight with my parents again. This time there was a party being given by one of my old friends who I had raced against during my Beetlecat days. His parents were off island, and he had the house to himself, so he decided to invite his friends over to party and drink. There was plenty of beer and hard liquor around. At one point in the evening, someone brought out a huge mug which held at least two bottles worth of beer. On its outside was written in red letters "I bet you can't." Filled to the top, I was challenged to chugalug the whole mug without stopping. I didn't hesitate. After I finished, there was applause and laughter. Despite the fact that I felt a little nauseated, I continued to drink scotch until midnight. When I left to drive home, I was very dizzy. Arriving home, I got out of the car and threw up in Mother's hydrangea bush near the front door. Waking up in the morning with a pounding headache, I swore I would never drink again.

These two incidents seemed normal and insignificant to me. Young people did such things. But they would turn out to be harbingers of days to come, when alcohol would change my life dramatically and take me down a bumpy path. The summer cruises with the Girl Scout mariners ended in September. I couldn't believe that in just two months the world cruise would start. My childhood dream was now on countdown.

With the summer cruise over, I went back home to Morristown and my parents. Two weeks after I arrived, Irving Johnson called and asked if I wanted to come up early to Gloucester, Massachusetts, where the *Yankee* was hauled out, to help Ed with the fitting out period before the departure on November 4th. I said "yes" although I knew it would cut down on my time with Mom and Dad from six weeks to two. When I left for Gloucester, I knew I would see them again, because they planned to be there on the big day: November 4th.

For a month Ed, Robert Johnson (Skipper's youngest son) and I worked hard. We bent new sails aloft, replaced old halyards and buntlines and renewed sheets and bowstrings. We spliced, served and parceled line. We painted the steel cap rail and varnished the skylights and big wheel aft. Despite my two summers of experience aboard, I learned even more from Ed and Robert. Ed came from an old, respected boat-building family on Cape Cod, and Robert had sailed on parts of previous world trips. They knew more than I did and I respected that.

At the end of the day, Ed and I would usually walk a quarter of a mile down the road to a local coffee shop where we would have supper. We'd talk about the day and the adventures that lay ahead of us. There happened to be a jukebox in the corner of the shop. We always played our favorite number of Fats Domino's "On Blueberry Hill." We liked the song so much that we sang it together while working. It could be anywhere, even high above the decks on the footropes of the foretopsail and foresail yards. We just loved Fats Domino.

During this busy period I managed to find time to sell my four-door Chevy. I can't remember who I sold it to, but I do recall the feeling I got after the new owner drove it away. With the sale, I had burned my last bridge. It was the final move to disconnect myself from my present life and free me up for a new and adventurous one.

The morning of November 4th finally came. The dock and *Yankee's* deck was crowded with family and friends of the crew. Mom and Dad, my brother Donnie, my mom's sister Aunt Eleanor and my godfather Gilman Low were all there. Despite the brave smile on her face, I thought I saw tears in Mom's eyes. She didn't want me to go, and I knew she quietly disapproved. It took me more years than I'd like to admit, to realize what a trooper she was that morning. She had visions of me graduating from Yale and becoming a businessman or professor. Now her son stood on the deck of a sailing vessel about to leave on a year-and-a-half cruise to God knows where with storms and other dangers lurking.

The moment came. At just before 11:00, *Yankee's* horn blared as Skipper requested that all guests to go ashore. In minutes, after hurried hugs with loved ones, we were left to ourselves. The engines started. The dock lines were let go, and we slowly drifted away from the dock amid loud cheers. It wasn't long before we were in the channel headed out to sea. As we worked our way down the channel, we passed at least a dozen commercial fishing boats tied up to the docks. They all blasted their deep-throated horns, and the fisherman waved to us. To top things off, three low flying F-86 fighter planes flew overhead in salute.

As we reached the outer channel and the breakwater, we started to set sail. My family had hired one of the many escort boats which followed us out, and my godfather took a photograph of me.

Then, as we passed the buoy marking the harbor entrance, one by one the escort boats turned around to head back. My family's boat was one of the last. But, finally, they too turned back with a last wave and a toot.

We were alone.

CHAPTER 4

ODYSSEY

Yankee's bow wake rumbled and hissed under a dark, starry sky. A brisk northwest wind blew off our starboard quarter, creating 20-foot seas and causing us to roll and surf down the front sides of large, curling waves. The old sailors called it "… having a bone in her teeth." We were two days out of Gloucester. It was 11:00 at night, and I was miserably seasick for the first, and what would be the only time in my life.

The crew had been split up into three watches of four hours each, 8:00 to 12:00, 12:00 to 4:00 and 4:00 to 8:00. We had eight hours off. Every Sunday the watches were dogged so that each would move up to the next four-hour slot. There were approximately six people to a watch.

Bermuda was to be our first port of call, and the week it took to sail there gave our inexperienced crew time to learn the ropes. There were many who had no experience at all. They quickly learned the basics: where the halyards, sheets and buntlines were; how to furl and set sail; how to go aloft safely; and how to steer a compass course. By the time we reached Bermuda, we were beginning to work the ship as a unit.

We stayed a few days, enjoying the motorbike tours and the beautiful beaches, before we left and sailed south towards the tropics and Haiti. The weather gradually moderated, and in a week we were in the trade wind belt. Here the winds blew constantly out of the northeast allowing us to keep all our sails set. Our square sails billowed out lazily, along with the staysails and main, nudging *Yankee* along at a leisurely 7 knots.

In the years since the cruise, I have often been asked what my favorite memory was. Many of the crew were asked the same question, and most of them said that our visits to Tahiti, Bali and other exotic places were their best experiences. But mine was different. It was when I was aloft as we ghosted under full sail. Here, for me, it was almost etheric. At 60 feet or more above the deck, I would comfortably sit on the foretopsail yard, lay my feet out on the swelling sail in front of me and lean my back against the foretopmast. Sails filled with wind were everywhere—above, below and on each side of me. Lines slapping against the mast, parrels groaning as we rolled, pennants snapping in the breeze, and the distant tumbling of our bow wake was for me the ship's orchestra and the music she played. And far in the distance lay the uninterrupted horizon above which usually floated puffy trade wind clouds.

Under full sail, we pressed on southward towards Haiti. Now out of the boisterous winds of the North Atlantic, the days became more subdued and peaceful. The crew continued to get better acquainted with each other. Of the 23 of us, four were women. Judy, Elaine, Put and our ship's doctor, Alice, would become our shipmate sisters in the months ahead. Their presence during future gales and rough conditions would have a calming effect. Then, of course, there was Skipper's wife, Exy, who, in her 50's, became the ship's "mother." She also spoke four languages, which would be invaluable later when dealing with foreign customs and immigration officials. The remaining 18 were young men whose average age was 21, except for Dink Barney who was 16. We all came from different parts of the country and some, particularly those from the Midwest, had never seen the ocean.

After sailing a week, we arrived at Haiti where we stayed for four days. It was a short stop, but long enough to see the terrible poverty, which was a shock for most of us middle-class Americans. The Haitian people lived in run down hovels rather than houses. The town Cap Haitian was dirty, and the streets were unpaved. Most of us were happy to leave.

With bunches of bananas hanging from our rigging, we continued towards Colon and the entrance to the Panama Canal, arriving there a week later.

Colon was a sailor's port. It had its share of tourist shops and restaurants but was also a hub for seedy bars and numerous "pleasure houses." Here, I must bring up an unspoken subject that has been avoided in all the publicity and books written about the Johnsons' voyages. Although we had six women aboard, including Exy, the rest of the crew represented a considerable amount of young testosterone. And when you have 18 young men who have been at sea for a long time, some of these houses of ill repute present a very real temptation. Colon was the first port to offer such enticements. There would be many more later on, such as Singapore, Bangkok, Capetown and Barbados.

One crewmember confided to me that in Colon he had found a place called the House of Love. It was an old, two-story estate home converted into a whorehouse. On the first floor there was a bar, dance floor and the women. On the opposite side of the bar was a stairway leading up to the rooms on the second floor. At the foot of these stairs was an old-fashioned cash register run by the madam. Whenever a customer wanted to take a girl upstairs, he would pay her first, and she'd ring him up, the old bell clanging for all to hear. The price for pleasure? A grand total of $7.50.

Skipper was not dumb. He knew this kind of thing went on and knew it was a necessary evil. He once told me he would rather ride out a storm at sea than spend one night worrying about his crew in a port like Colon. Luckily, nothing ever happened to anybody, and no one got into any trouble.

Our transit through the Panama Canal was uneventful. In Panama City we tied up and took on fuel and supplies, both of which would be unavailable for many months. Ahead of us was the Pacific Ocean, a body of water larger than the total land area of the earth. 10,000 miles stood between us and the next port where we could refuel and replenish our provisions. In the second week of December, we stood out to sea and entered the Pacific for the first time.

Five days and 620 miles later, we made landfall on the Galapagos Islands and spent Christmas anchored in a quiet, deserted cove at Isabela. Most of the islands had small settlements, but the archipelago was not geared to tourism as it is today. The unique aspect of the Galapagos was the wildlife. Though the Equator ran right through the middle of the islands, the cold Humboldt Current from the Antarctic caused an abnormally cool climate. Because of this, penguins, seals, albatrosses and other birds and animals thrived. Also, there were large Iguana lizards and the huge Galapagos turtle.

For Christmas and two additional weeks, we remained there while the crew hiked, dove for lobsters, which we ate almost daily, and shot small game. But, finally, the time came to set sail for our next destination which lay 3000 miles to the southwest and was still very much isolated from the world—Pitcairn Island.

The Jet Age has allowed us to travel quickly to any place on the planet. It takes only five hours to fly from New York City to Los Angeles and seven hours from New York to London. Yet, *Yankee* had to sail for 18 days to cover the same distance. This gave us an opportunity to experience a phenomenon the modern generation has never known—the marvel of distance. This was an unforgettable experience for me. There was something about sailing day after day surrounded by an unbroken horizon and empty sea. It was a moving environment consisting of waves, whitecaps and clouds. The only tangibles were the schools of dolphin we'd see once in a while and, of course, the ship. This was our world for weeks.

Shortly after leaving the Galapagos, we picked up the southeast trade winds. Each day we sailed before these winds, averaging 180 miles from noon to noon, and the crew settled down to the routine of sea life. As we had in the North Atlantic, we split up into three watches of six or seven crew members each, including Exy. There were one-hour tricks at the wheel with a mate in charge. If there was any doubt as to what to do in a given situation, the mate would ring a buzzer located by the binnacle (compass) which sounded below alerting Skipper who would be on deck in seconds. The only ones who didn't stand watch were Vic, the cook, and Skipper himself. During the night only the mate and helmsman were busy. The rest of the watch would be free to do anything they wanted, some catching naps, others just talking with one another. But they always had to be ready to act, if needed. During the day those not at the wheel would work. *Yankee* needed constant attention, and there were endless things to be done like painting, varnishing, splicing, rigging or sewing patches on ripped sails.

During our eight hours off, we read books, slept or played monopoly and cards. I used this time to write articles for the Nantucket Inquirer & Mirror, Nantucket's weekly newspaper that had contracted me to do 18 installments. Along with my long article which appeared in the Trinity Review magazine the year before, this would mark the beginning of my career as a published writer.

We had our meals in the main cabin at a long table which was on gimbals so that it always remained level no matter how much the ship heeled. It was strange to sometimes see those on one side eating their food at eye level while those opposite had their plates near their laps. What fresh food was purchased in port ran out after a week. The ship's galley refrigerator could only hold so much. For the rest of the passage, we ate canned food.

Every Sunday there was an informal church service held on the afterdeck. In the afternoon, Exy would have her Sunday tea party in the after cabin, inviting two different crew members each week. It was Exy's way of maintaining a small piece of civility in what was sometimes *Yankee's* rough and tough sea life. It also reinforced Exy's image on board as the ship's mother. We all felt we could comfortably confide in her and ask advice. She was a very special person who not only managed the provisioning of the ship, but also dealt with the customs officials in port. In addition, she was a very competent helmsman who took the wheel during all hands situations. It was interesting to see that Skipper was still very much in love with her even after 25 years of marriage. He often claimed he wouldn't have been able to successfully sail around the world without her.

We had a band on board, too. It was called Ed Crosby and His Baggywrinkle Boys. It consisted of two guitars, a banjo and a bass. The bass was simply a broomstick and a string attached to an upside down wash basin. Jeb Kreimer, who was to become my best friend on board, played guitar and was lead vocalist. I was backup guitar. Ed Crosby was on banjo, and Tom Keith played bass. We sang sea chanties and old songs like "You are my Sunshine" and, our favorite, "On Blueberry Hill," the classic Fats Domino song that Ed and I loved so much and first heard back during our Gloucester days. Our biggest moment as a band occurred later in a Bangkok night club when we were allowed to play during the regular musicians' break. We were not all that good because few people paid any attention to us. But at least we enjoyed it.

On the afternoon of January 26th, our 19th day at sea, I was sitting at my favorite spot aloft, on the foretopsail yard, as lookout. An hour earlier, Skipper and Ed had taken sun sights. and they calculated that we were 20 miles northeast of Pitcairn. With a lot of anticipation, I scanned the horizon ahead looking for the island. I hadn't been aloft long when I saw a dark lump interrupting the horizon off our starboard bow. For a while I stared at it, wanting to be sure I wasn't seeing things. But after 10 minutes the lump was still there, and I knew I was looking at Pitcairn. I didn't shout down to the watch right away because I wanted to savor the moment and have the island all to myself. But soon I couldn't contain myself. I shouted down "Land Ho!" In what seemed like an instant, the entire crew was on deck to see where I was pointing. At 500 feet high, and just a few square miles in size, the island rose steadily out of the sea as the afternoon wore on. Soon, we could make out the details of the dark cliffs plunging into the water, the white breakers smashing along the coast, and the green, rolling hills above.

As I stared at Pitcairn, I realized I was looking at history. It had been 168 years since the infamous mutiny on board the HMS Bounty. Its leader, Fletcher Christian, and is mutineers set Captain Bligh adrift aboard the ship's launch and then returned to Tahiti. Months later, taking 17 Tahitian men and women with him, Christian and the nine mutineers set sail again in search of an isolated island where they could feel safe from being discovered by the authorities. They found Pitcairn which offered what they were looking for. The island, with three smaller Islets not far away, lay 4000 miles west of South America, 1000 miles east of Tahiti and 300 miles east of the nearest island of Mangareva in the Gambier group. Burning the Bounty, the group settled on Pitcairn and were not found until 18 years later when the American trading ship Topaz visited the island in 1808. At that time only one mutineer was still alive. His name was John Adams.

I was familiar with Pitcairn's history and was more than anxious to go ashore.

But as night fell, Skipper decided to wait until morning. So we stood off the island for the night, none of us sleeping well, knowing that the next day we would be meeting the descendants of the Bounty mutineers and we would be staying with them for more than a week.

CHAPTER 5

PITCAIRN AND BEYOND

W HEN DAWN broke, we stood in towards the island. There was no harbor at Pitcairn. Instead, there was a small area called Bounty Bay, which was a misnomer. It could hardly be called any kind of anchorage. Three large boulders just 50 feet from the shore provided a slightly sheltered spot and partially protected it from the breaking surf. Offshore it was calm, and we were able to anchor a quarter of a mile away from the Pitcairners' boat sheds, which housed their 37-foot long boats, on Bounty Bay's beach. The Pitcairners had gotten up early to meet us. Launching all four of their long boats, they rowed out through the breakers, four oars to each side, and approached *Yankee*. With at least 20 islanders in each boat waving and yelling greetings, they came alongside, threw lines to us and scrambled aboard. I noticed their weathered tan faces, thick-lipped smiles and splayed out bare feet as they hugged us warmly like we were long-time friends. Within the first 15 minutes, Warren Christian, a direct descendant of Fletcher, had invited me ashore to stay with his family.

While we were there, the ship was to be left with a skeleton crew, allowing me to go ashore with him and spend a week with his family. After going below to get my things, I jumped into the longboat with him and his wife, Millie, and we were rowed ashore through the breakers and beached near the boat sheds.

I lived with Warren, Millie and their daughter Betty for the next 10 days. Life was simple and basic. There were no cars or vehicles, no stores and only a few electrical generators. A small post office, a meeting house and a Seventh Day Adventist church, which used the original bible of the *Bounty*, made up "downtown" Adamstown. A quarter of a mile up the slopes was a school run by Pitcairn's only foreigner, a teacher from New Zealand. All around, spread up and down the paths under the shade of the trees, were the crude wooden houses of 170-odd islanders.

Warren and Millie lived in a house on the fringe of Adamstown. Warren was wiry and quiet. Millie was robust, cheerful and outgoing. Given a cot to sleep on in their living room, I was made to feel part of the family. They had no electricity, so kerosene lanterns were used at night. A large outhouse in back was shared by all. Millie served tea at 7:00 a.m. every morning followed by a heavy breakfast at 10:00. Dinner was served at 6:00 p.m. In between, I spent some of my time helping Warren tend his vegetable garden up the hill from the house. Often we took long breaks and walked along the many paths which crossed the island and climbed up the hills. Once, we went to Christian's Cave, a place where, it was said, Fletcher Christian came to brood about what he had done — the cave overlooked the rich, blue Pacific 500 feet below — and I tried to imagine the feelings of guilt he may have felt about the mutiny.

There were two experiences I had on Pitcairn that I will never forget. The first was the arrival of a cruise ship on her way to New Zealand. Cruise ships passed Pitcairn occasionally and were the only contacts the island had with the outside world. The ships would drift a few miles offshore and allow the Pitcairners to come aboard to trade their carvings, weaved baskets and fruit in exchange for sacks of flour and sugar, commodities they badly needed on the island.

One cruise ship stopped while I was still ashore on the island. Heralding its arrival, a bell was rung in Adamstown, causing a frenzy of activity. Pitcairners, scurrying down the steep 500-foot path to the boat sheds and longboats, carried sacks of souvenirs and fruit to take out to the ship. I accompanied Warren, and soon we had rowed out through the breakers of Bounty Bay, with 20 other islanders, aboard one of the longboats. Once clear, the oars were shipped, and a primitive lugsail was set as we headed for the ship which was hove to a few miles offshore. In 20 minutes we were alongside the big ship, and a rope ladder was thrown to us. Loaded down with items, we struggled to climb to the deck above. Giving me a basket of avocados, Warren suggested that I go into the main lounge and see if I could sell any. As I entered, I saw many passengers sitting in comfortable sofas and walking around. I felt out of place with my straw hat, worn jean shorts and being shirtless and shoeless. I was aware of the strange sensation of the thick carpeting between my toes as I carried the basket of avocados. A number of people began approaching me wondering who I was. It soon was obvious that they were mistaking me for a Pitcairner, and I was asked several times if I was. I just nodded and smiled. For the next half hour, I became a bona fide descendant of the *Bounty* mutineers. I was also able to sell all of Warren's avocados.

The other experience that I will never forget was the chance to play a part in a historic find. It was well known that in 1790, in an effort to eliminate every sign that he and his band were hiding on Pitcairn, Fletcher Christian cut *Bounty's* anchor chain, drove her up on the rocks near Bounty Bay and burned her. Since that time generations of islanders, swimming in the area, had found copper nails strewn around the bottom. Then in 1933 Parkin Christian, the magistrate of the island, discovered the ship's rudder. And shortly before our arrival on *Yankee*, Luis Marden of National

Geographic had found pieces of copper sheathing, oarlocks, a dozen ballast bars and some fittings. But the *Bounty's* anchor had never been found.

Once during one of Skipper's visits to the island, he and Parkin Christian happened to be together looking off a high cliff which overlooked Bounty Bay. After a few moments, Parkin had pointed to a spot and calmly said, "That's where my great, great grand pappy's anchor lies." Skipper hadn't forgotten that time.

Now in 1956, we were having unusually calm weather at Pitcairn which allowed us to anchor the ship just a short distance offshore. We had four of the crew on board who were divers, and they had their aqualungs. During a particularly calm day, Ed, Buzz Fawcett, Chris Sheldon and Jeb were encouraged by Skipper to look for the anchor. Launching the *Yankee's* outboard with all their gear, and with me running the boat, we slowly motored over to the spot Parkin had pointed to years earlier. One by one the divers submerged to the bottom 100 feet below. I waited in the boat for 15 minutes until Chris suddenly broke the surface and said, "I think we've got it!"

What they had found was the fluke of an old anchor sticking out from the sandy sea floor. We tied a long line to it with a floating marker and then returned to the ship to tell the others. The news spread like wildfire, and by the end of the day, the whole island knew about it. Now the only question was how we were going to get it to the surface.   But Skipper had an idea. The next day, with a crowd of Pitcairners watching from the cliffs, he maneuvered *Yankee* directly over the marker. We lowered our anchor, and the divers below lashed it to the barnacled fluke. Carefully taking up slack, Skipper took advantage of the *Yankee's* rise and fall from the Pacific swells to gently tug the old anchor free from the sand. After half an hour and much difficulty, we managed to haul what was to be a 600-pound bower anchor. Later still, with tedious work, we were able to get the old anchor aboard one of the longboats where it was taken ashore and hauled up the boat ramps.

That afternoon all the Pitcairners came down to take a look at this link to their heritage. There was little doubt that it was the *Bounty's* anchor. We had scraped off some of the barnacles and found the imprint of the British Admiralty seal. We also found a number which later would confirm that the anchor had been registered to HMS *Bounty*.

Sadly, my stay with Warren and Millie ended, and I was once again aboard ship for departure day. It was an unhappy parting. The night before, under a huge banyan tree, the Pitcairners had given us a big feast of roast pork and fruits. Afterwards, we had played games and had fun into the night. Now we were heaving anchor to leave. After visiting the island every three years since 1934, bringing the islanders supplies and making friends, this was to be the last time. As we hauled our anchor up and started to set sail, the Pitcairners came out in their longboats and sadly watched. Then, with rich, moving voices, they began to sing the hymn "Bye the Sweet Bye and Bye." I looked backed at Skipper who was at the wheel. It's the only time I ever saw him in tears.

It was February 8th, 1957, when we left Pitcairn and set a course for the Marquesas, 1000 miles to the north. Skirting the Tuamotu Archipelago to our west, we only made one stop at Mangareva Island. Two weeks later, on the 22nd, we spotted the rugged peaks of Nuku Hiva rising out of the sea.

The Marquesas Islands were dramatically mountainous with cliffs and slopes falling into the sea to form fjord-like bays and harbors along the coastlines. Having five major islands, this group has been the subject for many writers through the years, including James Norman Hall, Thor Heyerdahl and Herman Melville. The latter actually sailed to Nuku Hiva on a whaler, jumped ship and lived with the Taipei natives for a year. His book *"Typee"* was the story of this adventure.

We anchored in Taiohae Bay on the south coast of Nuku Hiva where there was a small settlement consisting of a post office and a general store. The highlight of our visit was a ride by horseback up and over the high ridges overlooking the bay and down into Typee Valley where Melville had stayed. It was a remote area with a small village and friendly natives who greeted us warmly. Little did I know that I was to make this trip again in the future.

We left Nuku Hiva and stopped at Ua Pou for two days. Here, the villagers organized a soccer game and challenged our crew. As I recall, the game was tied in the first half but had to be called off because the soccer ball collapsed and lost all its air. It turned out this ball was the only one on the island! Our final stop was at Fatu Hiva where we enjoyed two days and where the islanders were constantly around the ship in their outrigger canoes.

Finally, we left the Marquesas and made for Tahiti, 800 miles to the southwest. Visiting Tahiti would be a milestone for me in that another one of my dreams would come true. During all those hours in the Groton school library, reading James Norman Hall plus the three books the Johnsons had written about previous world voyages, a second dream had been born, to go to the South Pacific and, particularly, Tahiti. Now, the island was less than a week away.

But on the third day of our passage, we were hit by a strong southeasterly gale which blew for four days. Standing watch on one of the blustery nights wet and cold, Tahiti, to me, seemed as far away as it had during my Groton Days.

CHAPTER 6

TAHITI AND THE PACIFIC

A DAY LATER the gale relented, and we sighted the outlines of the island's mountains in the early afternoon. Many have said that Tahiti is the most beautiful spot on earth. One author wrote that you were never completely the same after experiencing your first Tahiti landfall. We would soon see for ourselves.

During the next few hours, the island's outline became more distinct, and we were able to make out the details of 7000-foot peaks. In the late afternoon, the original blue color of the island transformed into emerald green. White waterfalls fell hundreds of feet from high plateaus into lush valleys. Eventually, after running before a brisk northeast breeze and closing the land, we saw coconut trees begin to emerge as they embroidered black sand beaches, and occasional clusters of grass-roofed houses appeared. By sunset we could see surf breaking as we made our way up the coast towards Papeete. When dark came, a gentle wind the Tahitians called the "hupe" wafted down the mountain slopes and out over the water, bringing the scents of tiare Tahiti and frangipani flowers. By 1:00 in the morning we were slowly powering through the large pass of the outer reef and dropped anchor off the town of Papeete.

I have never forgotten that day. It was when Tahiti put its mark on my soul forever.

With the wind in our faces, Jeb and I rode our rented scooters along the road which followed the 80-mile perimeter of Tahiti. Winding through the country districts, it was lined with tall, statuesque palm trees. To one side of us was the blue Pacific. On the other side were green valleys which transformed into gentle slopes reaching up to Mount Orohena and Mount Aorai. Frequently, we crossed rivers which originated at Lake Vaihiria, a crater lake 4000 feet above us in the central mountains. Crossing over rivers and streams spanned by wooden bridges, we often saw Tahitian women sitting in quiet pools washing their clothes. Sometimes we went through small settlements of grass-roofed houses where the people would smile and wave at us. But there were no stores or marketplaces until we reached the little town of Taravao on Tahiti's isthmus. After a lunch of fresh fruits and coconut juice, we continued around the island, going through districts with names like Mataiera, Papara and Punaauia. Our trip seemed like a dream. Everywhere, we saw incomparable scenery. When we returned to Papeete at dark, we were tired but happy. We had experienced some of the most beautiful environments we had ever seen.

Papeete was a different world, a town with a population of 20,000. Its highest point was the steeple of the Catholic church. The main street ran along the edge of the harbor separated from the water by a semi-circular quay. A few yachts, including *Yankee*, were anchored here with their sterns tied up to the quay's pilings. There were also three old copra schooners which were off-loading copra brought from the Tuamotu islands 300 miles to the northeast.

The tourist industry was practically nonexistent. There was no airport yet, and the only resort hotel was the Royal Tahitienne, a few miles outside of the town near Point Venus. The four-story Hotel Stewart was the one local hotel in town. Shops, small restaurants and bars were located on the side streets, and a large open marketplace did a brisk business in Papeete's center. The two popular bars, Quinn's and the Bar Lea, and the waterfront café called the Vahiria, opposite the quay, catered to the few foreigners on the island.

One thing I will always remember about Papeete was its traffic. There were a few cars, mostly French built Citreons, but the bulk of the traffic consisted of dozens of Tahitians riding their Vespa and Lambretta scooters, Solex motorbikes and bicycles. Omnipresent, open-sided buses offered transportation to the provinces, carrying bunches of bananas, papayas, coconuts, even bicycles, on their rooftops.

The Tahitians themselves were like all Polynesians, kind, easy going, friendly and fun loving. The men were handsome, the women were beautiful, and the latter practiced an interesting custom. If the younger women wore a single frangipani flower over their right ear, it meant they were married or had a boyfriend. But if they wore the flower over their left ear, it meant they were looking for a man.

The beauty of the island, the busy activity of Papeete and the friendliness of the people made for a memorable week. But after a week, we had to say goodbye. As we cast off our stern lines and headed out the pass, we set sail for the other islands of the Society group, which would include Moorea, Huahine, Raiatea and Bora Bora.

Taking a last look astern at Tahiti and the dominating Mt. Orohena, I somehow knew in my heart I would return.

In the last week of March, we left Bora Bora in the Societies and made for the southwest towards Tonga, 1200 miles away, stopping at Rarotonga, Aitutaki and Palmerston Island in the Cook group. As it had for the last four months, and would for the next year, the southeast trade pushed us westward as we set full sail, our log book showing we were making average daily runs of 170 to 180 miles. After a short stay in Tonga at the island of Nuku'alofa, we continued on to Suva, Fiji, 600 miles away.

It was during this passage that two of the crew came upon hard times. A day after we had set sail from Nuku'alofa, Don Alchin, who was our Olympic prospect in track, complained of back pain and stiffness. No one thought much of it, as we often developed strains and pulled muscles because of the hard work. But the next day Don's pain was much worse and Alice, our ship's doctor, examined him and immediately suspected he had polio. She was right. The following day Don became paralyzed on his left side. We isolated him in the forepeak, and Skipper contacted the authorities in Suva by radio about our situation. The local hospital was alerted and made preparations for our arrival. We reached Suva three days later. The paramedics were waiting for us at the dock. Don was hoisted ashore on a stretcher, put into an ambulance and taken to the hospital. Eventually, he would be flown back to the States and was never able to rejoin us. Unfortunately, Don has remained paralyzed to this day.

After he was taken ashore, we were put in quarantine and required to anchor in the harbor for the next 15 days. No one was allowed ashore, and each day a doctor came on board to check all of us out. It was with relief when the two weeks were over and we still had a healthy crew.

Ed Crosby, our first mate, was the other casualty. Ever since we entered the tropics in the Caribbean, Ed had suffered from quarter-sized boils which had broken out all over his body. Already a diabetic, these festering sores drained him of his energy and, by the time we reached Suva, he had over 100 of them. It was obvious that Ed needed medical attention. Ultimately, he was airlifted to Australia where he was treated and eventually sent home months later.

The loss of Ed and Don created a sad vacuum. When we finally left Suva, the crew set sail with heavy hearts.

Leaving Suva, we entered a new stage of the cruise. Having sailed 3000 miles across Polynesia, we were now headed for the New Hebrides Islands in Melanesia. These islands marked the eastern fringe of an area where the most primitive tribes on earth lived. Malekula, one of the biggest islands in the New Hebrides, still had tribes in the mountains that practiced cannibalism. Tribal hunters, wearing only penis wrappers and boar's tusk bracelets, hunted in the jungles with their bows and arrows, killing wild boar for food. Five days of sailing brought us into this new world as we spotted the mountains of Efate in the late afternoon.

As we stood off the shore at sunset, we could see columns of smoke coming from the fires in the villages. Some natives, rigorously paddling their outrigger canoes, tried to intercept us, turning back when they realized they couldn't catch up. We finally anchored late at night at Efate's only town of Port Vila.

What happened in the weeks to come was almost hard to believe. To understand this, I have to go back to World War II. At that time, the U.S. forces were building military bases as they fought across the Pacific. Some of the better known ones were at Guadalcanal and Iwo Jima. A lesser known one was the supply base at Espiritu Santos in the New Hebrides, called Vanuatu today. The presence of this base caused interesting and unusual reactions by the local tribes. Here were natives who speared fish and hunted wild boar in the jungle for their food, seeing for the first time jeeps, airplanes, guns, washing machines, radios and other conveniences of the modern world. Their reactions caused what came to be known as "cargo cults." A cargo cult was the belief of certain tribes that if the American GI had such things, they deserved them, too. On Tanna in particular, one of the most southerly islands, this belief grew into what was to be known as the "John Frum" movement. John Frum was a mythical sergeant who the islanders believed would return to Tanna one day, bringing all the modern conveniences the tribe needed. It was believed that he would come in a "great white ship."

John Frum had not yet arrived when we were in the islands.

Whether Skipper decided to visit Tanna out of curiosity about this movement or not, we'll never know. Whatever his reason, we left Port Vila and set sail for Tanna a few days later. A nice trade drove us at 10 knots, and in just two days we sighted Tanna off our starboard bow.

Whether by design or not, Skipper had all 8000 square feet of *Yankee's* white sails set. For the Tannese natives who saw us approaching, we must have looked like "the great white ship" bringing John Frum to them at last. It was soon obvious to us how serious they were because, as we neared our anchorage, dozens of wild looking natives in their outrigger canoes came alongside us in rows of three and four deep, excitedly shouting and gesturing. Some actually tried to climb aboard, and we had to gently restrain them.

At one point, a native reached out and handed Skipper a rolled up piece of paper. It turned out to be one of the strangest lists imaginable. On it were the names of certain Tannese and what items each one wanted. For instance, opposite one name was written "a P-40 airplane," another "a jeep," another "a rifle" and so on. Then one of the Tannese began chanting "John Frum, John Frum!" Skipper kept shaking his head and somehow convinced the group we were only emissaries, by speaking Pigeon English, a language they knew.

This unbelievable reception set the tone for the rest of our stay at Tanna. Whenever we went ashore, we were treated with much curiosity and respect. We were frequently followed by Tannese men and children who often attempted to touch us. On the other hand, the women seemed frightened. When we came into a village, many of them would be sitting at the entrances to their huts staring at us. As soon as we made eye contact, they would quickly disappear inside.

In one village the men were anxious to show us what appeared to be their

"John Frum Headquarters." It was a long, narrow grass shed. Hanging from the walls inside were combat rifles, GI helmets and old tattered American flags.

Frankly, we became tired of being treated like gods and tried to amuse them. One way we did it was through one of our crewmembers Jon Barney. Jon's feet looked entirely normal until you counted his six toes. We would call a native's attention to this by counting John's toes and then counting the native's. When the Tannese caught on, he'd count Jon's six toes several times, shaking his head and finally laughing. We had a lot of fun with Jon's feet during the entire cruise.

When we set sail and put Tanna behind us, we felt like we had just spent a week in a fantasy world. I felt relieved that, once again, I could be myself and no longer some cult figure. While I stood on the foot rope of the yard as we set the foretopsail, I watched the sail beneath me fill with wind and was happy to be back living my life at sea again.

My career as a crocodile hunter lasted one night. It happened at Tulagi in the Solomon Islands. It was early June, we had left Guadalcanal the day before, sailing the 20 miles across the famous "Slot," where the U.S. Navy clashed with the Japanese, and tying up to an abandoned World War II supply dock.

Tulagi was a favorite spot for crocodile hunters because there were so many mangrove swamps, the environment crocodiles loved. The market for belts, luggage accessories, wallets and shoes had always made hunting them a lucrative business. And there were some huge crocodiles around. One village had a 20-footer roaming the island for years. When the animal was killed and the stomach cut open, they found human bones. So there was always a certain amount of danger tracking these reptiles.

But killing them was easy. They were hunted at night, using small boats with outboards and a flashlight. Whenever there was a crocodile on the surface, the light beam would turn their eyes into two bright red dots, presenting a perfect target. The danger came in getting them aboard because they were still alive, flailing their tails and slashing with their sharp teeth.

One night, Jeb Kreimer, Buzz Fawcett and I decided we'd go hunting. I had brought a 30/30 carbine with me, the first gun I had ever owned. Tentatively getting it from my bunk, I went on deck and helped the others launch one of *Yankee's* small boats. For the next three hours, we slowly searched the mangrove swamps and inlets, getting lost in the pitch darkness many times. Deciding to take turns, we allowed ourselves three shots after which it would be the next person's turn. Using this system, we came up to many crocodiles on the surface, but they would always submerge before we got a good shot at them. Finally, during my turn, our flashlight beam picked up two red eyes, and I fired twice. This time the crocodile didn't submerge like the others. I had wounded him, and he lay motionless on the surface. Carefully, we grabbed his tail, hauled him aboard and gently laid him out in the bilge.

Suddenly, he started thrashing around, and we nearly capsized the boat trying to avoid his teeth. Then, remembering what the professional hunters did in such situations, we managed to turn him belly up and instantly he quieted down. By the time we returned to the ship, my six-foot trophy was dead.

It was 3:00 in the morning, and I crawled into my bunk wondering whether it had all been worth it. I was beginning to learn that I wasn't a hunter and hated to kill. Despite this, I would hunt one more time six months later on a safari in Africa.

CHAPTER 7

NEW GUINEA AND THE FAR EAST

NEW GUINEA is the second largest island in the world. You wouldn't think so by seeing it on a chart. But the Mercator projection makes it seem smaller than it really is. Actually, if you were to pick the island up and lay it along the east coast of North America, it would stretch from Nova Scotia to the tip of Florida, a distance of nearly 2000 miles. The rugged mountains of the Owen Stanley Range stretch down the middle of the island with the highest peak being 16,003 feet. Rocky cliffs fall into the valleys of dense rain forest and uninhabited land. There are two major rivers in Papua New Guinea: the Fly and the Sepik. Both are navigable upriver for over 200 miles.

When we arrived there in June of 1957, New Guinea was one of the world's few remaining frontiers. Some isolated tribes in the hills of central New Guinea practiced cannibalism and isolated incidents of head hunting were still reported. There were hundreds of tribes, many having different languages. In order to explore these areas, it was necessary to acquire a permit from the Australian government, absolving it from any responsibility for adventurous foreigners who might want to do some exploring.

The airplane was the major player for local transportation. Like Alaska, most of New Guinea's central highlands were inaccessible by land. If you wanted to travel inland, you had to hitch a ride on a cargo plane. These aircraft, for the most part, were old retreads from the two World Wars. The dependable DC-3 was the most popular because it could carry substantial amounts of cargo as well as passengers. These planes had no schedule. They flew where supplies were needed. Their pilots were called bush pilots because of the endless terrain of rain forests they had to fly over.

Our first stop was the town of Lae on the eastern end of New Guinea where we took on supplies. Then we continued up the north coast to Madang, a small port in which we planned to stay for three weeks. Our extended stay there would allow the crew to fly up to the highlands and Mt. Hagen. Here would be the starting point of an expedition into a remote area which was to be led by an Australian patrol officer who was familiar with the district.

I didn't go with them. Instead, Jeb, Tom and I volunteered to remain behind and watch the ship. Having *Yankee* to ourselves created an atmosphere of unaccustomed quiet and peace. Tom offered to cook while Jeb and I ran the generators. We relished the chance to sleep in late and because we had so much free time, we spent a lot of time ashore.

Madang was a small settlement with a few shops and restaurants. It had a picturesque town green where the Aussies played softball every afternoon. Being invited to play with them, softball became part of our routine. But it was the night I enjoyed most. The few bars in town attracted an interesting crowd including local bush pilots, coconut plantation owners and patrol officers. Over highball glasses of crème de menthe, a drink the Aussies loved, we listened to talk about the highland uncontrolled territories, stories of flying over the rain forests and discussions about plantation management. These characters had rough edges and thrived on their adventurous lives. They loved to drink, too.

Jeb and I kept right up with them, often staying until closing time. I drank every night and, despite waking up the next morning with a bad hangover, I'd do the same thing all over again. This was another sign, which I ignored, of what would be a serious drinking problem in the future.

But going to Madang's bars resulted in things besides hangovers. One night Jeb and I were talking to an Aussie named Adrian, who was a bush pilot working for a small outfit called Gibbes-Sepik Airways. He often went to Mt. Hagen, and it just so happened that he was making a flight there in the morning. He asked if we were interested in going with him. Without hesitation, we said, "Yes."

The next morning Adrian, accompanied by his 250-pound co-pilot Tim, picked Jeb and me up in a jeep, and we drove the short distance to Madang Airport. On our way I tried to imagine what type of aircraft we'd be flying and asked Adrian. He just smiled and said, "You'll see." I assumed it would be a DC-3. I wasn't prepared for what I saw when we arrived at the hangar in the back of the airport.

Our plane was an ancient tri-motored Junkers JU-52, a relic whose heyday was during World War II. It resembled the popular tri-motored Ford of the 1920's with wide, clumsy wings, a stubby tail section and a nose which drooped slightly. The plane should have been hanging from the rafters of the Smithsonian Institute rather than flying over the jungles and mountains of New Guinea.

Despite our misgivings, the Junkers actually lifted off the runway gently as it carried a 7-ton cargo of canned food. Sitting in the jump seats, we watched the dense, green rain forest below stretch out for miles without a sign of a village or a human being. Over the noise of the engines, Adrian explained that most of the 200,000 natives lived in the central valleys beyond the Owen

Stanley Range. After an hour of steady climbing at 120 mph, we looked down at the canopy of trees as they thinned out and gave way to bare patches of rock that gradually rose up ahead of us. Finally reaching an altitude of 10,000 feet, we flew through a pass between two mountain peaks and descended into Goroka Valley on the other side. Green plains and gently rolling hills showed cultivated plots and large farms, and we passed small villages whose inhabitants waved at us.

Soon we were making our approach to Mt. Hagen's airstrip. Unpaved and running slightly downhill, the runway was at an altitude of 5000 feet, making it one of the highest and most dangerous landing strips in the world. Using his expertise as a bush pilot, Adrian brought the Junkers down for a hard landing and a final abrupt stop. Then we taxied to a small structure that served as a terminal. As we taxied, a group of Papuan tribesmen waited for us and when we had cut the engines, they began unloading our cargo.

They were wild looking. Flat-nosed and tall, they wore mother-of-pearl shells that dangled from their noses and ears. Others had headdresses of bird of paradise feathers. While unloading our cargo, they excitedly talked back and forth to each other using primitive, guttural words. It was a surreal scene. We were looking at people who had rarely, if at all, seen a television set or a washing machine or a tractor. Instead, they belonged to the past. They hunted wild boar with spears, cultivated their land with crude hoes and rakes and had shrunken heads dangling from the ceilings of their grass-roofed huts. When we returned to Madang later that afternoon, Jeb and I felt that we had been in another world.

It was in Madang where I received what I have come to refer to as the "Coconut Letter." It was sent to me by Medford Kellum, an American who owned a coconut plantation on Tahiti's neighboring island of Moorea. We had anchored opposite his waterfront home, in Papetoai Bay, with a stern anchor and our bow lines tied up to the shoreline trees. Papetoai Bay was one of two beautiful bays on the north coast of the island. There was a village a few miles from Kellum's home, but the rest of the land in the area was taken up by his plantation.

After I had explored its considerable size, Kellum told me the plantation was for sale. This interested me. I had the money, and buying land would fit in nicely with my desire to return to Tahiti. It would also allow me to become a permanent resident who wouldn't have to renew a nine-month visa repeatedly. The last day we were there, I told Kellum I was interested and asked him to write a letter describing the plantation and what he was asking for it.

Now, back from the Goroka Valley adventure, I sat down and read the letter:

Dear Mr. Williams:

As we agreed, I'm sending you this letter to inform you I am definitely selling my property here in Moorea. Its total area is 1510 hectares or approximately 3500 acres. I'm asking $156,000.

This land is one continuous piece with well-defined boundaries. It has over 400 meters of water frontage on Papetoai Bay. The title is absolutely free and clear of any claims or mortgages. There are very few properties here that can be bought by foreigners in French Oceania. This is one of the largest and most desirable on the market.

Opunohu Plantation has about 4000 fully bearing coconut trees which produce 25 tons of copra annually. There are also 450 head of excellent beef cattle, with good barbed wire fencing, 6 vanilla plantations and thousands of producing lime, breadfruit, orange and pomplemus trees. In addition, my coffee plants produced more than a ton of dried coffee this year.

Also there are a number of freshwater streams in all valleys which flow year around. In these streams are an abundance of shrimp and many fine trout which take a fly nicely.

Sincerely,

Medford Kellum

I knew I wouldn't ever find a more ideal place in paradise than Kellum's plantation. If I did buy it, my plans to go back to Tahiti could turn into a lifetime in the Pacific with a substantial income, as well. My return, which I had vowed to make, was looking like much more of a reality. Putting the letter safely in my bunk, I tried to get my mind back on the cruise.

We left Madang the last week of June and headed north towards the mouth of the Sepik River 250 miles up the north coast. The Sepik is the longest river in New Guinea, winding 700 miles up to its source. It was navigable as far as 200 miles where there was an outpost settlement called Ambunti. Hot, humid and ridden with mosquitoes, the river had villages which were built alongside its banks. Often, the inhabitants paddled out to us offering clay pottery and carvings as we slowly powered upstream. We traded for these items with t-shirts and sticks of tobacco which Skipper had expressly brought for this purpose. At night we anchored mid-stream, trying to sleep in the oppressive heat while fighting off the continuous attacks of mosquitoes. They were so thick that the natives ashore had to roll themselves up in pandanus mats at night to avoid being constantly bitten.

A few days later, having gone upriver 175 miles to the settlement of Ambunti, we returned downstream to the wide-open sea. Relieved that we were able to breathe mosquito-less air again, we set a course to the west once more. I remember it was July 13th, my 22nd birthday.

Having sailed almost 12,000 miles of the Pacific Ocean in nine months, we spent the next three months touring the Far East. Entering the Celebes Sea and stopping in Borneo, we continued across the South China Sea to Bangkok where we stayed for two weeks. Here, Jeb and I took a well-deserved break and checked into a hotel for a few days. Then we continued sailing south, laying over in Singapore before resuming to sail south through the Java Sea and finally to Bali.

Of all the places we visited in the Far East, Bali was hands down my favorite. It must have been Skipper's, too, because we stayed there for three weeks, our longest time in port during the world cruise. Bali was one of the most beautiful islands in the world. Almost 100 miles long and 60 miles wide, it had a population of close to 3 million people. The central mountains of the island were over 6000 feet high, the most dominant being Mt. Agung, which was an active volcano. Terraced rice fields and farms formed patterns on the mountain slopes, and winding roads connected the coastal and inland villages. The largest town was Denpasar where small pony-drawn carriages, with Bermuda bells as horns, served as taxis.

The Balinese were steeped in tradition and their culture. Hindus for the most part, they practiced a variety of customs which were unique. Colorful dancing characterized many of these customs. Many of the dances were done by young girls dressed in elaborate costumes and headdresses. One dance the men performed, was called the Monkey Dance which consisted of a chorus of voices emitting loud guttural grunts resembling monkeys while the other men of the group danced and gestured.

The highlight of our visit was a huge cremation ceremony which was held in the inland village of Ubud. It was the funeral of a popular Hindu priest who had died 30 years previously and whose remains had been kept in a small box in his family's home.

A 40-foot bamboo tower had been built, its frame covered with multi-colored decorations shaped as wings and buttresses. These decorations were made of compressed coagulated rice. The priest's ashes were placed in a compartment near the top of the tower. The tower's framed base was a 20 x 20-foot platform built of sturdy bamboo poles.

On the day of the cremation, hundreds of people from the nearby villages came to Ubud to participate in the ceremony. Then the unbelievable happened. At the appointed time, 30 strong men lifted this heavy tower to their shoulders and began to slowly move forward. As they did, the tower precariously leaned to one side and then the other while the carriers groaned under its weight. With dancers and onlookers following behind, the huge tower, with its human beasts of burden, was carried down the road for a few hundred yards and then returned, coming back to the original starting point. Chanting dancers now circled it as the carriers struggled under its enormous weight. There was even one man who climbed up onto the platform and waved a white flag at different spots in order to chase away any bad spirits which might be around. Finally, the exhausted men eased the tower down to the ground and set fire to it.

On the morning of October 24th, we weighed anchor and left Bali astern. We had gone halfway around the world. Now we were about to enter the Indian Ocean. Our destination was Mombasa on the east coast of Africa. Ahead of us would be one of the finest passages of the cruise and would be 37 days of unmatched sailing.

CHAPTER 8

THE INDIAN OCEAN TO AFRICA

I stood at the wheel and tried to keep *Yankee* on a straight course. Anticipating sudden shifts in direction, I spun the helm one way, then the other to counteract, while at the same time bracing myself as the ship rolled. It was, as Skipper often said, "like keepin' her on the head of a pin." We were a few days out of Bali, and the 20-knot southeast trade was blowing off our port quarter.

The day before, we had broken the ship's longest noon-to-noon record run by logging 250 miles. Now, there was a possibility of breaking it again.

Our Indian Ocean crossing gave us some of the best sailing of the world cruise. Being at 7 degrees south latitude, we were in the heart of the trade wind belt, just as we had been in the Pacific. Day after day the wind blew from the same direction, hardly varying a degree. Except for the rare rain squall, the skies remained clear with the familiar small fair weather clouds hovering just above the horizon.

After our long stay in Bali, I was happy to get back to sea. We easily settled back into *Yankee's* special world as we stood watch, did deck work and maintained the rigging aloft. I was particularly busy with the ship's navigation.

Skipper had begun teaching us navigation when we were on our 19-day passage to Pitcairn Island. It was his intention that we learn so that in the future, all the mates would be capable of working out the ship's position each day. By the time we entered the Indian Ocean, most of us had become reasonably proficient at this. I didn't know at the time that what I was learning would become indispensable to me later on.

As I had learned during the summer cruises, the sextant measured the number of degrees the sun was above the horizon. Applying this to the navigational tables and Greenwich meantime, I was able to come up with a line on the chart. The ship would be somewhere on that line. These sights were taken mid-morning.

At noon I was able to get a second line on the chart by calculating our latitude by roughly using the same method. I then knew the ship was somewhere near where the two lines intersected. This was called a "running fix," which was usually within 5 miles of our true position.

Celestial navigation was more accurate. Skipper taught us the names of all the important stars and where they were. After some practice, I was able to identify many stars, such as Sirius, Canopus, Rigel Kentaurus and Capella. I'd take sights at dusk when both of the stars I chose and the horizon were visible at the same time. Doing that gave me two different intersecting lines showing *Yankee's* position where they crossed. This was more accurate because both sights were taken at the same time, unlike during the day when they were taken hours apart.

And then there were the watches. Being 3rd mate, I had my own watch which included one of the women. One good thing about having either Judy, Put or Elaine on watch with us was that they always prepared hot cocoa at night using a small hotplate in the lazarette behind the wheel. This was especially appreciated when we were in bad weather. More importantly, however, the women provided that special female energy which had a calming and comforting effect on us men.

I loved the night watches the most. Without the artificial light pollution generated in cities and residential areas ashore, the stars lit up the black sky with startling clarity. At times you could even see faint shadows on the deck because of the starlight.

And the full moon was still more captivating as it cast a dreamy, shimmering path on the water.

As I have written earlier, most of the watch chose to sleep on deck while one hand took his or her one-hour trick at the wheel. The mate watched for any changes in weather or wind direction. During the day the whole watch turned to and worked on whatever had to be done. Rigging aloft was spliced and served, patches sewn to repair sails and painting done around the deck.

Happily, we had the chance to rest, too. Eight hours off watch gave us plenty of spare time. Often, I would spend it sitting in my favorite spot aloft, 50 feet above the deck on the foretopsail yard, where I could take in the magnificent scenery around me. Up to the present day, 50-odd years later, I have never been to any church ceremony or meditation group where I have felt more peace of mind and connectedness to the present. With silent, billowing sails around me, I was in another world. Sometimes I would stay up for hours, only to climb down on deck reluctantly to retire to my bunk.

There was, however, a certain monotony in doing and seeing the same things day after day. Fortunately, this monotony was occasionally broken by certain incidences. One was the appearance of abundant schools of flying fish. We had seen them every once in a while since we had left Bermuda, but the Indian Ocean seemed to teem with them. They would catapult themselves out of the water and glide downwind for 50 yards or so with their tails trailing the surface. Usually flying in twos or threes, they always ended their flights with dramatic splashes. Some of these fish had the misfortune of flying over our bulwarks at night, and we would find some in the scuppers during the morning watch. These were picked up and handed down the galley skylight to Vic who would fry and serve them for breakfast.

Every so often we were joined by schools of dolphins, too. They were an absolute joy to watch. Playful and acrobatic, they would jump clear out of the water as if to say, "Look at me!!" I would always climb out on the bowsprit to watch them swim just below the surface ahead of our bow wake. There was one night when we were sailing through water which had a high phosphorus content. It made the submerged dolphins look like erratic torpedoes, darting this way and that.

Another monotony breaker were the few times we were able to put our boat over the side and take photographs of *Yankee* under sail. It had to be a day when the trade was light enough to allow our small outboard to keep up with the ship. This was an exciting opportunity because the person who sees his ship least often under sail is the one who is on board sailing it. Then, in our small outboard, we were able to go out a quarter of a mile and ahead of *Yankee* to see her gracefully running towards us with her 11 sails set. The photographs we took that day were worth a thousand words, but being there was worth ten thousand.

A month and a half at sea, we arrived in Mombasa the first week in December. We were to remain there for 10 days, during which two expeditions had been planned. The first was an ambitious attempt to climb the 20,000-foot Mt. Kilimanjaro. The second was a hunting safari in Kenya, 80 miles up the road towards Nairobi near Tsavo Park. Despite my one night's wretched experience as a crocodile hunter in the Solomons, I signed up for the safari along with Buzz and Mike. The lure of spending seven days and nights camped on the African plains was an opportunity I couldn't turn down.

Our professional hunter and guide was an Indian named Ikram Hassan. I had the vision of an African hunter as having a rugged build and wearing a pith helmet with a pipe dangling from his mouth. Hassan was far from that image. Instead, he was slight, wore glasses and looked more like a college professor. He was one of only two Indians in the profession. He had been a professional hunter for 15 years and was considered one of the best.

The team consisted of three Kikuyu Africans, Hassan and the three of us. The natives were 85-year-old Munifacki, the skinner; Bishi, the cook; and Mongali, the tracker. Our vehicle was a one-and-a-half-ton safari truck specially designed for hunting. A gun rack was located in the back of the front seat. Behind was another seat that accommodated three people. Above was an open hatch that allowed someone to stand up and watch for game as the truck was being driven. In the far back was a large area used to store equipment and any game that we might shoot. Each side of the truck was open so that anyone, at any time, could quickly jump out and shoot.

Early one morning we left Mombasa and headed north on one of the only roads which linked the city with Nairobi 300 miles away. After 10 miles we turned off onto a pot-ridden dirt trail. Bush and trees prevented us from seeing any distance for some time. Finally, after a few hours, our view opened up as we came to a rise. Before us lay the vast African plain which stretched for miles in a sea of green and brown. By late afternoon we had driven 80 miles and stopped to set up camp near a stream, a short distance from the road. Two tents were rigged, and a wooden table was placed in the middle of the camp's clearing.

When dark came we lit a fire, ate dinner and drank rum. Occasionally, a lion would roar in the distance and hyenas nearby grunted with their strange laughing barks. The scene was unreal, and I felt like I was part of a page written by Ernest Hemingway.

For the next six days we fell into a routine. Early in the morning we would climb in the truck and drive through the surrounding plains looking for game. We weren't able to hunt for the big animals, like lions and rhinos, because our stay in Kenya would be too short. At the time, to get a big game license, we would be required to reside in Kenya for six months. So we settled for small game permits which allowed us to hunt the smaller animals, like hartebeest, Grant's gazelles and zebra. In the process, however, we would be able to see the big animals, like elephants and giraffes.

We followed a rule. Whosever turn it was to shoot stood above the truck's roof in the hatchway. When game was sighted, that person hopped out of the truck and took a shot. If the animal was only wounded, the shooter would quietly follow Mongali, the tracker. They would sneak through the grass until they found the animal, kill it with a second shot and then drag it back to the truck. The second day, I killed a Grant's gazelle which was grazing in an open area 150 yards away. I hated killing it so much that at the end of the day, I put my rifle away and never used it again on the safari.

During the week we saw all the big game except elephant. The giraffes fascinated me the most. When they stood still, they looked ungainly and awkward with their 20-foot necks. But when they ran, they transformed into graceful horses galloping in slow motion. We saw lions also, and they seemed unusually tame, remaining where they were as we passed near them. This was probably because Tsavo Park was nearby, and the cats were accustomed to human beings. Often, we encountered water buffalo and rhinos but, unlike the lions, we gave them a wide berth.

At night we relaxed around the table while Munifacki skinned the animals we shot during the day. Bishi cooked zebra and gazelle meat for supper, and afterwards we drank by the fireside as Hassan told us stories about Africa and his hunting experiences over the years.

For nearly a week we lived the safari life and saw a genuine part of wild Africa. But time ran out, and we had to head back on the rough road to Mombasa again. Reluctantly saying goodbye to Hassan and the Kikuyus, we returned to the ship. Once aboard, we traded stories with the Kilimanjaro group. Three had made it to the top, including Put, but the other four didn't because of altitude sickness.

At last we set sail from Mombasa and headed for Madagascar and the Mozambique Channel 500 miles to the south. With us we took memories that will last for a lifetime.

The hurricane's squalls literally screeched through our rigging. Winds of 100 mph pinned us against the topgallant yard as Tom and I struggled to tie extra lashings around the sail. Although we were 50 feet above the deck, some of the crests of waves rose above us as the ship fell into the troughs in between. *Yankee* rolled so wildly from one side to the other that we were forced to hold on with both hands. The old sailor's saying "one hand for the ship, one hand for yourself" wasn't applicable. It was more like two hands for the ship or two for yourself. Even the driving rain stung the backs of our necks. With all this tumult raging around us, I felt helpless and insignificant.

It was two days after Christmas, and we were midway through the Mozambique Channel, a body of water 300 miles wide that separated the southeastern coast of Africa from the island of Madagascar. We had heard reports on the radio Christmas day about a hurricane with 135 mph winds near its center that was moving directly towards us. Being in the Channel, we had little room to maneuver to get out of its way.

The next day the sky had become overcast, and dark squalls lined the horizon. We ran before an increasing northwest wind and driving rain and were forced to take in the foretopsail, then the fisherman staysail and, finally, the inner and outer jibs. By midnight the storm had reached hurricane force, and all hands were called to take in the mainsail. When morning came, the ship was wildly racing before huge waves 100 yards apart from each other, looking like hills more than swells. The *Yankee* rolled so wildly that she was taking on water over her bulwarks which sloshed back and forth and floated some of the lumber stowed on the port side deck. Torn from their lashings, these planks dangerously swished one way and the other until we were able to relash them.

Now safely back on deck, Tom and I made our way carefully to the afterdeck and watched Irving at the wheel. I saw no fear in his face. Instead, there was an excitement as if he were enjoying the chaos around him. But soon he was faced with a tough decision.

Despite having shortened down to just the main stays'l and forestays'l, *Yankee* was still tearing before the huge seas at 9 knots. The problem was we were running too fast. This increased the danger of us broaching to; that is, unavoidably veering broadside to the wind and waves and being thrown on our side. If that happened, we could sink. By mid-afternoon Skipper made his decision. We had to heave to, a maneuver which required rounding up and facing the wind. This would allow *Yankee* to drift before the gale with her bow heading into it. He called all hands again and, with difficulty, we took in the mainstays'l leaving only the forestays'l set. Then he waited for a lull in the following seas and, when it came, steered hard to starboard. We spun around into the wind with the forestays'l steadying us. Now, with the wheel lashed, the ship alternately rounded up into the wind and then fell off. In such a position, *Yankee* merely drifted slowly with the elements instead of racing before them.

After making sure we were properly hove to, there was nothing left to do on deck. We went below and let the *Yankee* take care of herself. All that night the wind howled as we tried to sleep, occasionally poking our heads outside the main hatch to see what was going on in the fury outside.

On the third day, the storm began to abate. In the afternoon we were able to square away and sail before the wind again. By nightfall we had reset the fisherman, fore topsail and jibs, and we tore through the water. Someone mentioned it was New Year's Eve. We had been so preoccupied with the storm we hadn't realized it. By midnight the clouds began to break up in the southeast and stars appeared. It was exhilarating as we raced downwind at 10 knots, away from the hurricane and into the year of 1958.

Rounding the Cape of Good Hope, one of the stormiest areas in the world, was mild compared to the hurricane we had passed through earlier. The only discomfort was the cold, which we hadn't experienced since leaving Gloucester. At 35 degrees south latitude, temperatures were in the 40's with raw winds and cold water, forcing us to wear heavy coats and watch caps. What

I'll remember most about the Cape were the majestic wandering albatrosses who seemed to follow us for days. Having a 7-foot wingspan, they gracefully soared just above the wave tops, rarely flapping their wings. To many sailors, along with the "bosun's bird" (Tropicbird), the albatross meant good luck. And good luck we would have for the remainder of the cruise.

On January 17th, we entered Table Bay in Capetown and tied up to the main pier. We would remain here for two weeks until we departed for our last leg of the world cruise and home.

CHAPTER 9

HOMEWARD BOUND

A FTER ENJOYING the hospitality of the Johnsons' Cape Town friends, we set sail at the end of January and began the long passage up the South Atlantic. Once again, the crew settled down to the familiar routine of sea life, some happy about it and some wishing we had stayed a little longer. But our mindset was a little different this time because we realized we were finally headed home after over a year of sailing and that it would all be over in the next few months. I found myself appreciating each day under sail and, more than before, trying to savor the moments.

Almost every passage had a new experience for us, and this one was no exception. We were to set the studding sails for the first time. Stunsails, as the old sailors called them, were kite-like extensions set beyond the yardarm ends. There were two of them set, one above the other. The best way to understand what they are is to look at the paintings of the clipper ships. In most of these paintings the ships have their studding sails set, flying out beyond the regular square sails. These sails could only be set in light winds. Fortunately, there were a few times when we were able to put the boat over and get photographs of the ship with these sails set. They presented a beautiful sight. Any one of the pictures we took could have been aptly entitled "Under a Cloud of Sail."

We also went through another experience of a very different kind. One of the only downsides of the trade wind belts were the squalls which developed from time to time. When we sailed through one, it generally lasted 10 to 15 minutes and was accompanied by torrential rain. But some of these squalls also had wind, and we never knew how much until they hit us. Some generated winds of gale force which were dangerous to a sailing ship. There was only one way to predict how intense these squalls were. If you could see through them when they were still at a distance, the winds would be light. But if they looked like a black wall, then be prepared for a real blow. This rule of thumb is clearly reflected in what an old sea captain was supposed to have said to his mate, "If you can see through 'em, Mister, hang on to your tops'ls." But if a ship under sail was caught by sudden high winds, it was imperative to put her "off," which meant running before the breeze to lessen the strain on the wooden masts.

One day, a particularly threatening squall approached us from windward. At the time, we had all our headsails set including the jib topsail, a sail whose stay runs from the bowsprit tip all the way to the top of the foretopmast. (This fragile wood spar is a vertical extension of the larger steel foremast below.) As the squall approached, the wind off our starboard bow began to increase, and *Yankee* started to heel sharply. The watch was ready to put her off as Skipper came on deck. But he didn't give the order. Instead, he looked aloft at the foretopmast as the wind blew harder. Minutes later, the squall was howling through the rigging, and the *Yankee* raced through the water in turmoil of rain and spray. Glancing aloft again, Skipper noticed the foretopmast bending from the strain of the pulling jib topsail. Only then did he order us to bear off before the wind. But it was too late. There was a sickening snap, and the mast broke in two, causing the jib topsail to collapse into the water to leeward along with much of its rigging.

After the squall had passed and things calmed down, we got back on course and began to clean up the mess. Sheets, halyards, sail and wires trailed in the water, and it took us half a day to untangle the mess. *Yankee's* two remaining jibs remained intact, and under all plain sail we continued on our original course. It would be weeks later in Barbados where we would have a new fore topmast fitted to replace the old one.

After the fact, some of the crew believed Skipper had wanted to see how much the foretopmast could stand. Others, like me, guessed he was waiting for the mate to order the ship put off before the wind. But when he realized the mate was, in fact, waiting for him instead, it was too late. Whatever the reason, it marked the first time anything like that had happened in the thousands of miles we had gone around the world.

A few days later, at approximately 5 degrees south latitude, we lost the southeast trade. It was significant to me because I had spent so much time studying the history of sailing ships and knew the trade winds had played a major role in the world's commerce. Without these dependable winds, cargo-carrying routes from New York to San Francisco, Honolulu to Singapore and Cape Town to the West Indies would have been much more difficult to sail. And these winds were free fuel. That's why on that day I became somewhat philosophical and wrote these thoughts in my diary: "Sunday, March 2, 1958 — In the middle of my watch this afternoon, we lost the southeast tradewind. The southeast trade!! How many miles had it pushed us? Thousands: 7000 miles across the Pacific, 4500 miles across the Indian Ocean and 3000 miles up the South Atlantic. That was a total of almost 15,000 miles! It seemed as though it should have left us with a little more fanfare."

But it didn't. Instead, it was replaced by a quiet calm interspersed with rain squalls. We were now in the doldrums, an area on both sides of the Equator characterized by calms and variable winds.

Two weeks later on March 16th, we sighted Barbados and, again, I wrote in my diary: "Land! A strange, unfamiliar obstruction of the sea's horizon which had been empty for weeks. At 2:00 a.m. this morning the island's twinkling lights became visible, one by one, and before dawn we were sailing along the coast towards Bridgetown. The scent of land was wafted out to us by a soft offshore breeze. How wonderful it is to smell land again! People who have never been to sea cannot comprehend or appreciate such an experience. It's almost like a rebirth of your senses.

"We dropped anchor in 5 fathoms of water as dawn was breaking. Then, a police boat came alongside and asked where we had come from.

"'Capetown,' replied Skipper, '45 days out.'"

Realizing our unique world voyage was coming to an end was a downer for everyone. This sadness began when we left Barbados and reached Nassau in the Bahamas. Here, some of the crews' parents had flown down to meet us.

Mom and Dad, accompanied by my godfather, were among those parents. We had a warm reunion and all went out and had dinner one night. I recall regaling them with stories of the voyage. But what I remember best was after dinner, when my godfather and I walked through a park nearby and talked. I had always found it comfortable to confide in Gum - a nickname we used because when I was young, I couldn't pronounce "Gilman"

- and expressed to him my love for Tahiti and my wish to return there. I told him about the possibility of buying Kellum's coconut plantation in Moorea, something I had never mentioned to my parents. After listening, he encouraged me to follow my heart's desire but also cautioned me to think things through before I made any decisions.

Finally, we had departed Nassau, saying "goodbye" to our parents, knowing we would see them in four weeks. We arrived in Bermuda a week later and spent a few days touring the island on motorbikes and diving in the crystal clear water. Bermuda was our last port. Reluctantly leaving it astern, we had then set a course for New York City.

For five days we had sailed north until we made our New York landfall. It had been unreal, sighting the tall skyscraper of Manhattan. Under power, we worked through the narrows and proceeded up the harbor past the Statue of Liberty and towards lower Manhattan. I remember looking curiously at the new model cars, including the strange Ford Edsel, moving along the Beltway. And as we entered the East River, I gazed at the Empire State and Chrysler Buildings towering over us. After Tahiti, New Guinea and the South African plains, they looked like giant 100-storied Goliaths.

From New York we had leisurely worked up the coast, gone through the Cape Cod Canal and now were drifting off Gloucester on our last night.

At the completion of our cruise, Irving and Exy Johnson had made seven trips around the world, more than anyone else then or now. And it was amazing at first look that Skipper, after sailing for a year and a half on each cruise, always returned to Gloucester exactly at the time he promised he would, 18 months earlier. But this was not as difficult as you might think. His secret was to arrive off the port's entrance a day or two early and then mark time by drifting until the morning of the scheduled landing at Gloucester's dock. This way he could easily time our 11:00 a.m. appearance almost to the minute.

So, as in the past, we found ourselves 3 miles off Gloucester's channel the night before it all ended. Having nothing else to do, the crew gathered in small groups on deck and below, reminiscing about our adventures and experiences. There was a tangible sadness among all of us. I don't think any of us slept much. Finally, at 10:00 the next morning, Skipper headed into the Channel and, before a large crowd at the Rocky Neck dock, ordered our lines made fast and the engines shut down. The world cruise had at long last ended.

That night a big party was thrown for the crew and their families at the home of one of the Johnsons' friends. There was dancing and speech making, and even our musical group "Ed Crosby and His Baggywrinkle Boys" played to the amusement of everyone. The next day we said goodbye to each other and then climbed into our cars and left in different directions. My dream from childhood had run out. It was unreal and the finality was hard to accept.

CHAPTER 10

IN LIMBO

For me, the next eight months would turn out to be a period of unease and restlessness, where I found it difficult to readjust to normal life. For one thing, there was the pressure coming from my parents to go back to college and choose a conventional career. My closest intention to this was the idea of maybe becoming a writer/photographer for National Geographic Magazine. But my other goals would ultimately earn me the family's official title as its black sheep. This was reflected in the wish to buy my own schooner and sail on a voyage similar to *Yankee's*. My other unconventional goal was to return to Tahiti and buy Kellum's plantation, a drastic departure from the norm.

After my return I spent the summer on Nantucket with Mom and Dad. During this time I put a lecture together using some of the many Kodachrome slides I had taken over the last 18 months. I also had dramatic 8mm footage of the hurricane we had sailed through in the Mozambique Channel. I felt I could put something together that would interest people, and public speaking appealed to me.

As a result, I presented half a dozen lectures that summer. Two were held at the American Legion Hall in town, two more at St. John's Episcopal Church on Fair Street, one at the Nantucket Yacht Club and several informal showings in friends' homes which drew 15 to 20 people. They were all a success and I enjoyed doing them. But I quickly realized that any plan to go on a major tour was unrealistic. My films were not 16mm, which was necessary for a large screen with a large audience. And I hadn't taken enough footage anyway.

Then, as September approached, I was faced with the problem of whether to go back to college or not. Going back was the last thing I wanted to do. My free-spiritedness was too strong. The possible schooner cruise and owning a plantation in the South Seas easily overcame any more sensible decision like graduating. But as things happened, the decision was made for me. On meeting with the Trinity College registrar, I was told I lacked the necessary credits that were required. I would have to go to summer school almost a year later before I would be admitted as a junior. I didn't want to wait that long.

So I decided to go to Oahu and check out the University of Hawaii. This plan would kill two birds with one stone. I would be doing a sort of half return to the South Pacific while going ahead with my education at the same time. I expected a lot of resistance to this new plan from Mom and Dad, and I got it. But when they saw that I was determined, there wasn't much they could do. With resignation in their faces, they watched me pack and then sadly wished me well.

I arrived in Honolulu and found a small apartment to rent near Waikiki Beach. After a week of settling down, I went to the registrar's office at the University of Hawaii.

Looking at my records, they told me exactly the same thing Trinity had. I can't say I was very disappointed. As a matter of fact, an excitement grew when I realized I was free to do what I really wanted to do.

Now, my focus was completely on whether I should buy Kellum's plantation. I wrote Kellum telling him I'd like to come down to Moorea to seriously consider buying his land. He responded right away, inviting me to come as soon as it was convenient. So I called Mom and Dad and told them. It was the first time they were even aware I was interested in buying a coconut plantation, and it must have been an enormous shock to them. This was the second time in four months that I had delivered a bomb shell.

In December I bought plane tickets to Tahiti. Unlike today's direct flights, I had to take a 707 to Suva Fiji and then transfer to an antiquated World War II PBY flying boat. Owned by Teal Airlines, this was the only way one could fly to Tahiti because there was no airport there at the time.

I boarded the plane at Honolulu and spent the long flight nursing the expectations running through my mind. Landing at Suva, I transferred to the PBY, and before I knew it we were touching down into the quiet waters of Punaauia in Tahiti.

I had returned to Paradise.

CHAPTER 11

UTOPIAN INTERLUDE

I sat on a knoll, in the shade of a tree, as I looked out at what could be my future domain. Most of Kellum's 3500-acre plantation and Opunohu Bay was spread out before me. Endless rows of coconut trees lined the beaches, and open fields covered gentle slopes where cattle grazed. Mount Tohivea, Moorea's highest mountain at 4000 feet, towered over the still bay. Nowhere was there a sign of human presence.

I was lost in thought while I gazed at the scene around me. It was very hard to believe that my determination to buy the plantation had died. A week earlier I had received a telegram from my concerned brother Donnie urging me to reconsider buying the land. He was worried about me depleting my trust fund. And there was something else bothering me. I had been staying with the Kellums in their comfortable house near the water for a week. Now, finally confronted with actually buying the plantation, doubt had begun to creep in as to whether or not I was doing the right thing. I was getting cold feet. Would I be happy exiling myself from mainstream life? What would it be like to be surrounded by thousands of acres and have no one to talk to?

There was another thing that bothered me. Was I using the purchase of Kellum's land as just a means to live in the area indefinitely? Or might it be a rationalization to convince myself I had a goal, some kind of an excuse to validate what I was doing? Each day I had been mulling these things over. I had taken walks alone through the plantation. I had watched workers gathering copra and maintaining the vanilla fields. I had climbed up the hills that overlooked Opunohu Bay. Did I belong here or was I isolating myself too much?

After 10 days, I told Kellum I had changed my mind. Not surprisingly, they agreed it was a good idea. They confessed to me that all the time they had been reluctant to sell to a 24-year-old only to have him tire of the life and sell the plantation to some unknown buyer.

I returned to Papeete confused, wondering how I could have been so taken up by my enthusiasm for so long to buy Kellum's land only to lose interest in it in a matter of days. It was a blow to my confidence and trust in myself. I needed some distraction to get my mind off of it. So I decided to stay out what was left of my nine-month visa and, perhaps, start a book or write some articles.

I found a small grass-roofed bungalow right on the beach six miles from town. It faced Matavai Bay with Point Venus in the background where 168 years ago Fletcher Christian and his band of mutineers had anchored the HMS *Bounty*. Having a sand floor and pandanus windows held open by bamboo sticks, it was 600 square feet, had a bedroom and what might be called a small living room. The rent was $35 a month. For transportation, I bought a new Vespa scooter.

Once settled, I began writing an article about Tahiti and also composed a long letter to Mom and Dad telling them in detail why I hadn't bought the plantation. At night I scootered into town and went to either one of the two popular bars in Papeete. Quinn's had a world-wide reputation, and it was there you were liable to meet some of the Europeans who were in town. But I liked the Bar Lea best, a smaller place which featured genuine Tuamotus music played by Tuamotuans themselves on guitars and ukuleles. Here, I would spend hours listening to the music and watching fun-loving Polynesians enjoy themselves. And I watched the Tahitian women, too.

As I had learned during our *Yankee* visit a year before, I knew which women were available and which weren't. I remembered that wearing a flower over the left ear meant they might be looking for a partner. Little did I know one night that this guide would lead me to my first love, a milestone no man forgets.

That night I noticed a Tahitian girl sitting alone at the opposite end of the bar. She was strikingly beautiful with long, flowing raven hair, soft features and a warm smile. Right away I saw that she was wearing a flower over her left ear. I stole glances at her for quite a while, thinking how nice it would be to have a girl like her. I wanted to approach her and introduce myself, but I had always been a dismal failure at picking up women.

But she saved me the trouble. When I finally got the courage to make eye contact with her, she smiled, left her stool and came over to me. She introduced herself as Rose, gently putting her hand over mine. She was a pure-blooded Tahitian with sparkling brown eyes and a fun-loving nature. After an hour of conversation, we both felt that we had known each other all our lives. At closing time we left the Bar Lea together. Climbing up on the back of my Vespa, she wrapped her arms tightly around me with her chin on my shoulder, and we rode home to my bungalow.

As things would have it, she spent the night and didn't leave for the next eight months.

Almost every day we took long rides into the provinces to visit her relatives or to sightsee. We went to countless inviting swimming holes in many of the island's rivers. Some of these pools were so deep, we could dive into them from the river bank or from an overhanging tree. Often, Rose brought our laundry along which she washed in the shallow streams. Then while holding hands we would quietly wait for the clothes to dry as we took in the natural environment around us.

Rose was also a dancer who was part of a troop that performed at the island's sole resort hotel called the Royale Tahitian. I would watch fascinated as she danced to the fast rhythms, shaking her hips as if they had ball bearings. A friend of mine once jokingly claimed that Tahitian women had universal joints in their hips.

Most nights we went to either Quinn's or Bar Lea. Sometimes I would have too much to drink. Whenever that happened, she would drive the Vespa home with me clinging to her on the back seat. Once or twice we even went fishing with my landlord who had his outrigger conveniently hauled up on the beach near my bungalow.

This time in Tahiti with Rose was one of the happiest in my life. There were two periods, however, when I reluctantly left her to go sailing for a few months.

Away for six weeks, I sailed as a passenger aboard the copra schooner *Vaitere* as she went to the Tuamotu islands 300 miles to the northeast to collect copra for the Papeete market. Copra is the oil yielding meat of the coconut and is the prime export of the South Pacific islands. At one time there had been many sailing schooners working out of Papeete. But by then the *Vaitere* was one of the few remaining.

The Tuamotu archipelago is a group of 78 atolls stretching 700 miles from southeast to northwest. They are extremely low islands whose highest points are their coconut trees. Because of this, during landfalls the first thing you see is the tops of these trees which appeared to be growing right out of the horizon. Each island is a circular rim of land with a lagoon in the center. Some have passes leading into their lagoons, others don't.

Besides copra, other exports of these islands included oyster shell and pearls. The island lagoons were rich with oyster beds, and the shells were used to make buttons, earrings and knife handles. And in some oysters pearls were found which were very marketable. Harvesting oysters was done by divers who, without underwater breathing apparatus, would dive to depths of 100 feet and stay under for two to three minutes. Each year the diving was planned at a different atoll to conserve the oyster beds.

Having no passenger accommodations whatsoever aboard the *Vaitere*, I slept on deck along with a dozen other Tahitians. Our first destination was the island of Takaroa. Sometimes under sail, but most of the time depending on the schooner's old diesel engine, we arrived at the island's pass in three days and tied up to the village dock to load up copra.

The *Vaitere* was to remain two days, then leave and stop at eight more islands before she returned to Takaroa on her way back to Papeete. This gave me an opportunity to stay on the island for a few weeks and experience Tuamotuan life for myself. Fortunately, on the first day I met a Takaroan named Ramana who had invited me to come and sleep with him and his family. I remember him being very apologetic.

"We have little here," I recall him saying. "Our water comes from whatever rain we have. Our food is coconut and fish and the beds are hard. But we welcome you."

His house was very much like my grass-roofed bungalow in Tahiti. Small with only a few rooms, it served as home for him, his wife and two small children. Early every morning Ramana would go diving in the lagoon with his homemade spear gun. It was made of carved wood from the islands, a steel point manufactured in France and a heavy elastic band from the island's one Chinese store. He always returned with a string of fish which his wife would clean and cook on hot bricks. Ramana and his family made me feel at home with their Tuamotuan lightheartedness and carefree spirits.

Physically, Takaroa was a typical atoll in the archipelago. Its lagoon had a 12-mile circumference and in many places was more than 100 feet deep. The lowland circling it was no more than 100 yards wide a profusely covered with coconut trees. There were no cars or scooters. A wide, coral sand path rand down the middle of the village and was swept periodically by the women with palm fronds. Grass huts lined each side of the path, and there was a Mormon church and a Chinese store directly across the way, the lagoon beaches were quiet and provided ample space for the outrigger canoes to be hauled onto the sand near the village dock. And the trade winds constantly rustled the coconut palms day and night.

It was at night when the Takaroans' love for life and music manifested itself most. When it became dark, you could hear the sounds of guitars and ukuleles everywhere. As I walked down any path, I would invariably run into a group strumming and singing. The groups could usually be found under a coconut tree where they would strum ukuleles and create syncopated rhythms on wooden drums. One evening, I got the courage to bring my own $10 guitar, which I had bought in Papeete, and I was taught how to play the fast beat of Tuamotuan music.

The weeks rushed by, and before I knew it, the *Vaitere* was back and ready to leave again. Saying goodbye to Ramana and his family, I boarded the schooner, as her lines were cast off and she backed away from the dock. As this was happening, I heard the popular song of "Vini Vini, Vanna Vanna" being sung by some of the islanders. It took a second for me to realize they were singing to me—that they knew my name was "Win" and had appropriately picked that song. I didn't know that I would eventually return to Takaroa to hear them sing it again.

Despite my interesting visit to Takaroa, it was good to get back to Tahiti and Rose. I didn't have any way of knowing I would soon leave her once more. One day shortly after my return, I was in Papeete driving along the waterfront when I noticed a graceful 100-foot schooner whose topmasts towered above the other yachts. Anchored with her stern facing the bulkhead, I saw the name *Wanderer* beautifully carved on her transom. And coiling a length of line was a tall Viking of a man with a shock of disheveled hair. I recognized him right away as Sterling Hayden, the Hollywood movie actor.

I asked him if I could come aboard, and he waved his hand in invitation. Sterling had been Irving Johnson's 1st mate on the first world cruise back in the 1930's. This created an instant connection between us, and we ended up talking for an hour. Before I left, he asked me if I was interested in sailing with him as a deckhand for the next few months while he sailed to the neighboring islands. It didn't take a second for me to think about it. I said I'd love to.

When I got home and told Rose, she half smiled and said "aita pe'a pe'a" which was Tahitian for "never mind." But I saw sadness in her eyes. With some reluctance, she helped me collect my clothes and offered to take care of the bungalow while I was gone.

Three days later I was helping the crew let go *Wanderer's* lines and haul the anchor. We were bound for Taha'a, 80 miles to the northwest. After setting sail, I had a chance to meet the crew. Sterling's 1st mate was Spike Africa, a well-known schooner man from Sausalito who was accompanied by his wife, Red. The rest of the crew was a study of diversity. There were two Americans, a German, two Chileans, a Tahitian cook and Sterling's three children.

The presence of these children wasn't explained to me until later. Sterling had, apparently, defied a court order when he sailed *Wanderer* out of Sausalito months earlier. In a messy divorce proceedings with his wife, he was ultimately awarded custody of his children, provided he wouldn't take them out of the country. He assured the court that he was only "going to sail down the coast to Santa Barbara." But Santa Barbara was never to see him or the *Wanderer*. Instead, he cleared the land and set a course for Tahiti, 3500 miles to the south. He had defied the court and literally kidnapped his own children. It occurred to me that, being a part of his crew, I might be an accomplice to his act. I had no idea that a year later Sterling would apologize to the court and be let off scot-free.

We sailed to Taha'a, Raiatea, Bora Bora, Huahine and Moorea, returning to Papeete for short periods between trips, which allowed me to have warm reunions with Rose and my bungalow home. On one of these returns, Spike and his family had to leave and return to California. Suddenly, I found myself promoted to 1st mate.

Cruising the Society Islands with Sterling was another unforgettable chapter in my life. Under sail, he was completely in his element. Along with Irving Johnson, Sterling was the most capable sailor I have ever met. Years ago, he had been the main topmast man for the famous fishing schooner *Gertrude Thebaud*. Later, he had gone around the world on the *Yankee* and then eventually got his master's license. Finally, he had bought the *Wanderer*, which was originally a bona fide lumber schooner which worked the West Coast in the 1890's. Living this full a life, it was a wonder he was able to fit in a Hollywood acting career.

He was definitely a better sailor than an actor. It was true he had starred in Marilyn Monroe's first movie *The Asphalt Jungle* and later Stanley Kubrick's *The Killing*. He had also been in many Westerns as a sheriff or outlaw. Once, one of these movies was playing in Papeete's only theater. It was his idea that we all go. I found myself watching him on the screen, yet, sitting next to him, as well, listening to his frequent remarks about his bad acting.

To me Sterling was a misplaced master of sail who had the misfortune to have been born in the wrong century. I would often watch him at the wheel when we were under sail, as the schooner heeled and raced through the water. He seemed to blend in with the scene and become part of it. The schooner and her crew was his only world. What he so often described as the superficiality of Hollywood's world was far away and forgotten.

The clearest memories of my time with him were the nights when we anchored in an island's quiet lagoon. With a background of surf pounding on the reef and a starry sky, Sterling would light a kerosene lantern and hang it from the main boom aft. Then he would go below and return with a bottle of rum. As we drank, he would, in his low-pitched, dramatic voice, recount stories of his escapades or complain about the shallowness of Hollywood life. It was times like this when we felt we could solve the problems of the world. And the rum only enhanced these feelings.

We had been sailing to the out islands and returning to Papeete for almost three months. One night, when we were anchored in one of these dreamy lagoons, Sterling asked me something.

A moon path glimmered on the water, and we had been drinking rum.

"Why don't you do it yourself?" I remember him asking.

"Do what?" I said.

"Get your own schooner."

I had thought of this many times before. Why not? I had the money. I had the time. I had the experience. I could make long voyages to the Pacific, shoot films and lecture afterwards like Skipper had. Sterling went on to say he knew the perfect person in Los Angeles for me to meet. She was a friend and yacht broker who could easily find the right schooner for me. Her name was Peggy Slater.

My own schooner! Yes! Sterling had set my free spiritedness on fire. A week later when we had returned to Papeete, I left the *Wanderer*. Sterling wrote a letter to me months later saying he had been sad to see me go because I was "the best damn schooner man" he had ever sailed with.

It was hard leaving Sterling. It was even harder leaving Tahiti, but it was heart wrenching leaving Rose. That last week we were inseparable, savoring every minute together. When the day came and I was boarding the old PBY bound for Suva, we hugged each other on the dock and cried. When I boarded the plane, I took one last look at her. She had thrown a lei of tiare Tahiti flowers into the water.

I felt a sudden ache in my stomach because something told me that I would never see her again.

CHAPTER 12

FIRST COMMAND

I walked into Peggy Slayer's San Pedro office on a Monday in August. Introducing myself to the receptionist, I said I was a friend of Sterling Hayden's and was looking for a schooner to buy. As we were talking, an imposing, red-haired woman appeared at the entrance of the back office and listened quietly. She studied me curiously, and I knew it was because of my disheveled hair and the informal clothes I was wearing. Then she gestured to me to come into her office and invited me to sit down.

I came straight to the point and explained to her exactly what I was looking for—a 40-foot gaff-headed schooner with a clipper bow and a raised afterdeck. At first, she said nothing and just stared at me. Then she smiled.

"I know of one," she said. "She might be what you're searching for, but she's expensive."

"That won't be a problem for me," I answered. I remember she gave me a doubtful look and then opened one of her desk drawers and pulled out a photograph. It showed a black-hulled, salty-looking schooner which was gaff-rigged with a clipper bow. Peggy said the owner was asking $50,000 and that the schooner was located up the coast in Santa Barbara and would I be willing to drive the 70 miles up there the following day.

Years later, Peggy wrote a book about her life as a yacht broker for the celebrities and Hollywood stars. In it she wrote of our meeting. At first, she admitted she was skeptical, describing my young, unkempt appearance. She thought I was a dreamer with no money but decided to humor me anyway.

The next day we drove up to Santa Barbara. When we arrived at the yacht anchorages on the waterfront, Peggy didn't have to point out the schooner to me. I immediately knew she was the vessel lying at her mooring a short distance from the main pier. A smaller 45-foot version of Sterling's *Wanderer*, she was a model of the old coasting schooners which sailed the West Coast 75 years ago.

We went out to her in a launch and Bill Clarke, her owner, was there to greet us. After introductions, he gave us a tour. Her name was *Marie Celine,* and she was everything I had imagined. Beneath a jutting bowsprit was a graceful clipper bow. Aft, she had a raised deck surrounded by a taffrail, and her square stern was beautifully carved. Aloft, she boasted a main topmast from which a main-topsail and fisherman staysail could be set. Her decks were teakwood; her planking, Philippine mahogany and her sails, dacron. Below was a large cabin forward with a Shipmate stove, four bunks and a forepeak. Aft were two wide bunks and a roomy navigational area with a large table top in the main companionway hatch. Between the cabins was an ample head and the engine room with a GM diesel.

We hadn't been aboard 20 minutes when I agreed to buy her. I told Bill I would call my financial advisor in New York and that he would wire the money within two days. It was as simple as that. Peggy never had an easier client. A week later I had my first experience sailing *Marie Celine* as the three of us brought her down the coast to California Yacht Anchorages in San Pedro where Peggy had reserved a slip for me.

Once settled there, I called Mom and Dad. This was something I had put off for as long as possible, knowing it was going to be another one of those unexpected shockers just like the coconut plantation was the year before. Dad's first question was what plans I had with the boat. I explained I was sailing back to Tahiti and was working on finding a publisher who would be interested in a book about the voyage. Beyond that I couldn't elaborate. There was a long silence at the other end of the line. Finally, Dad asked a few more questions and then urged I update them on what would be going on. We talked a little while longer and then hung up. I was left with the feeling that Mom and Dad had, once and for all, given up any thought of my living a conventional life like Donnie, who was already a practicing attorney.

However, with a bit of luck, it wasn't long before my plans transformed and took a more definite direction. I knew that the pearl diving season in the coming spring would be held at Takaroa in the Tuamotus where I had had the two-week stay with Ramana the year before. So on a hunch, I contacted *National Geographic* magazine and informed them I would be sailing there and asked whether they might be interested in an article. There was a response from them almost immediately. They were interested in the idea and asked that I send a brief sample of my writing. I did and they liked it. This resulted in signing a contract with them. It specified that I would arrive at Papeete the following March, pick up staff photographer Bates Littlehales and then proceed to Takaroa and work on an article. I was ecstatic.

This was a huge windfall. Now, in my mind, my voyage to Tahiti seemed justified, not just solely a personal desire to return. So I planned a departure for early February, giving me ample time to reach Papeete by March. It would also allow me time to find a crew and fit out the schooner.

Right away I began preparing for the trip. The first, and most important thing, was to familiarize myself with *Marie Celine's* sailing characteristics. I wanted to know how she would handle in every situation. To do this, I invited Peggy and her friends to go sailing with me on weekends. We cruised to Long Beach and other coastal ports as well as Catalina, 24 miles offshore. I practiced approaching and departing anchorages under sail. I tested the schooner's limits during windy days by setting as much sail as I thought she could stand. I heaved her to in order to see how she'd respond and, for the same reason, jibed and tacked her dozens of times. Finally, I docked her every chance I got to see how she handled under power.

At the same time, I looked for a crew. I felt that three, besides me, would be enough. Eventually, I found Don Heinz, an engineer for Raytheon, who was willing to take a year's leave of absence from his job. Because he was a friend of Bill Clarke and had had experience sailing on *Marie Celine* before, I made him 1st mate. Then I asked two likeable 19-year-olds named Mike Rae and Jack Crone. Mike was the son of a scientist. In contrast, Jack's father was a former Idaho potato farmer.

Jack's family was hesitant to let him go because, at 26, they thought I might be too young, and they wondered if I had the necessary experience. So they invited me to their Long Beach home for dinner one night, obviously, for the purpose to check me out. Over supper, I recall telling them stories about my time on *Yankee* and my days with Sterling Hayden. After we ate, I laid out a chart of the South Pacific on their kitchen table and showed them just where I planned to go. Mike's parents were an easier sell because his father was a friend of Peggy Slater who, by that time, had sailed with me many times aboard *Marie Celine*, and she vouched for my abilities as a good sailor.

Provisioning and fitting out was time consuming. Besides all the rigging that needed replacing, I had to purchase enough food to last us for at least two months. There were the essential items like spare line, marlin, varnish, paint and new sails. I found a secondhand Plath sextant for $90 at a marine supply store, and I ordered charts, H.O.214 tables and pilot and tide books. But you can't think of everything. One week before departure, I figured we had everything we needed until I realized I had forgotten pencils, for plotting, and toilet paper.

Christmas came and went and February 3rd, the departure day I had chosen, was coming on quickly. I had the schooner hauled at a nearby boatyard to have her bottom painted. By chance, Irving Johnson had just given a lecture in Los Angeles at the time and dropped by San Pedro to take a look at *Marie Celine*.

"She's a proper vessel," Skipper remarked with enthusiasm after taking a thorough look at her. "She'll take you anywhere you want to go."

In my mind, *Marie Celine* had just been given the ultimate seal of approval.

The morning of February 3, 1960, finally arrived. The day was clear with a light west southwest wind. Friends were crowded around the slip, as we cast off our lines, and I backed *Marie Celine* into the channel. As an escort of half a dozen boats followed, we set the main, fore, forestaysail and jib. In 30 minutes we were abeam of the breakwater, and the wind had shifted to the northeast and freshened, allowing me to add the main topsail and fisherman staysail. The schooner heeled to the breeze like she was free at last, and I set a course which would bring us around the south end of Catalina and out to sea. One by one, the escort boats gave a last wave, turned and headed back. By early afternoon we were alone.

It was all surreal. Well south of Catalina Island, we were clear of the land and heading on a course directly into the sunset. Here I was, 26 years old, sailing my own schooner to the South Seas with a crew of three—one, an engineer; one, the son of a nuclear scientist and the other, a son of an Idaho potato farmer. My destination was Nuka Hiva, more than 3000 miles away. Life didn't get much better than this, I thought.

Twenty-four hours later, it was a very different story. During the night the northeast wind had increased to gale strength, the barometer had plunged and threatening clouds hung over the horizon. The once gentle seas we had off of Catalina and San Clemente islands the day before had turned ugly, and all three of my crew were seasick.

By noon that day I determined we had sufficient sea room and bore away to the south before the wind. Now *Marie Celine* rampaged through the water like a racehorse. Sliding down the front sides of large 30-foot waves, we reached speeds of more than 10 knots, and it became obvious the mainsail had to be taken in. While I struggled at the wheel to prevent us from broaching to, the crew fought the sail to gather it in. After a long battle they managed to lower it and lash it securely with gaskets.

Now, without the mainsail's steadying effect, we rolled wildly from side to side, causing pots and pans to crash to the floor in the galley below. On some of the bigger rolls, solid water came over the rail and flooded the decks, tearing things loose and drenching the deck generator. All we could do was to tie everything down and hold on. Before dark we had to take in the fisherman staysail and jib, leaving us with just the foresail and forestaysail.

Before midnight it was blowing full gale, and I knew we had to heave to. Sheeting in the two sails tight, I waited for a lull in the seas and then spun my helm hard to starboard. The schooner responded and rounded up her bow into the wind. Things immediately quieted down. Now, giving way to the storm rather than racing before it, the schooner drifted almost broadside to the seas, slowly working her way up towards the wind and then falling back to her original position again. There was nothing left to do but close the hatches tight and go below.

Compared to the storm's racket, it was strangely silent inside. We sat around the forward cabin table looking at each other, and I saw concern on everyone's faces. I tried to make light of things and managed to convince them that we were fine and not to worry. Then, on the pretense of going on deck to check the wheel lashings, I climbed through the hatch and out into the storm again. But I didn't look at the lashings right away. Instead, because of the stress, I went to the lee rail and got sick over the side.

In my misery, I was learning that one of the most difficult things a captain has to do is hide his fear from the crew. It was imperative I was a source of confidence, not anxiety. I had never felt this responsibility so strongly. As mate aboard *Yankee*, all I had to do in a serious situation was to ring a bell located near the wheel, and Skipper would be on deck in seconds to relieve me of any decision-making. There wasn't a bell on *Marie Celine*. Everything was in my lap. I was the man. I took a deep breath, returned below and told the crew to get some sleep.

The morning of our third day out, conditions moderated somewhat, allowing me to square away before the wind once more. For the next few days, we sailed south while the crew, now over their seasickness, began to work as a unit. Jack cooked hot meals every day while Don and Mike helped me out on deck. And to my great relief, everyone began to learn the knack of steering the schooner before the seas. For me this was a Godsend because ever since we left San Pedro, I had been at the wheel almost constantly and had not slept. Now, I could go below for short periods and get some rest, knowing the guys would keep us on course.

The overcast and fresh winds persisted for the entire first week, preventing me from getting any sun sights to work out our position. I had to rely on dead reckoning, a method of determining an estimated position by using the average speed and course of the vessel. On our seventh day out, I calculated we were at approximately 22 degrees north latitude and 122 degrees west longitude. This meant that we had travelled an average of 140 miles a day and were close to 1000 miles southwest of San Pedro.

At this point we were cold and tired after so many days of rough weather. Any romantic notions about sailing to the South Seas had been replaced by shivering reality. But on the eighth day, things began to turn. A warming sun came out, and the wind lightened to the point where we were able to set full sail. Spirits rose, particularly mine because I knew we had probably caught up with the northeast trade winds.

Our second week at sea seemed to want to make up for the first. Warm, tropical east northeast winds filled our sails and caused endless whitecaps on the surface. The familiar cotton ball, fair weather clouds floated above the horizon all around, and the sea took on a sparkling blue. The decks dried, and we were able to hang our laundry out in the rigging. Sail handling became rare, sheets untouched. Schools of flying fish under our bowsprit erupted out of the water, gliding over the wave tops ahead of us. At night our sails were dimly outlined against the darkness, and the stern wake hissed quietly. Stars seemed to touch the schooner. The Southern Cross appeared above the horizon, its base always pointing to an imaginary spot on the horizon that was exactly magnetic south. That allowed whoever was at the wheel to keep *Marie Celine* on her desired southerly course without even looking at the compass.

We saw no other ships, no aircraft. Our days were measured by the series of circled dots on the chart. These represented the noon positions I had worked out each day by taking sun sights in the morning and noon and star sights at dusk. We averaged a quiet 130 miles a day.

At the start of our third week, we were at 3 degrees north latitude, or about 180 miles from the Equator. Here, we ran out of the northeast trades and entered an area of calm the old sailors called the "doldrums." Then the southeast trades came, and we hauled our sheets and continued to the south on a close reach.

In the late afternoon of our 21st day out of San Pedro, Don saw a Blue-footed Boobie flying low over the water off our port bow. This was a significant sighting because I knew these gannets were land-based birds who ventured as far as 150 miles offshore. This was the first concrete sign of the accuracy of my navigation. My noon sight five hours before had shown we were 120 miles north by east of Nuku Hiva, our Marquesas destination. The next morning another sign of land showed itself in the form of a bobbing coconut. I was quietly excited. I knew we would see land that day.

My guess was that we would sight Nuku Hiva's 4000-foot mountains by noon when we were 50 miles away. But noon came and went with an empty horizon. At 1:00 I sent Mike aloft to get an elevated vantage point. He saw nothing. By 2:00 I was getting nervous. We should have sighted the island by then. I began thinking that my figures had been wrong and I had been making the same mistake day after day, putting us a hundred miles east or west of the Marquesas. Then, with enormous relief, I heard Mike yell.

"Land Ho!!"

"Are you sure?" I shouted back. And then I saw it too—a dim outline of undulating, bluish mountain peaks on the horizon. I was exuberant. I had done it! We had sailed 3000 miles in 22 days, and now our destination was in sight. It was one of those moments in life you never forget. A year later, Dad, who had been more than unenthusiastic about me purchasing *Marie Celine*, was to write a letter to the editor of the *Nantucket Inquirer and Mirror* describing this voyage to the Marquesas and signing it "a proud father."

As the afternoon wore on, Nuku Hiva's mountains transformed from faint blue to rich green. Then deep ridges and sculptured valleys appeared as we got nearer. At sunset we were close off the eastern shore of the island where we saw coconut trees and black beaches. After so long in a constantly moving environment, the land by contrast seemed wonderfully motionless.

As it was growing dark, we arrived at the southeast corner of Nuku Hiva, and I jibed the schooner over and headed west along the south coast. It was near midnight when we entered Taiohae Bay, a deep fjord-like harbor surrounded by steep, bold ridges. At the head of the bay, I let go of the anchor in 20 feet of water.

For a few moments, all of us were silent as we listened to dogs barking on shore and smelled the land. The passage had ended, and I gratefully looked at my crew. A moment later I went below and reappeared holding a bottle of Cutty Sark that I hadn't told them I had aboard. Then, stringing a kerosene lantern from the main boom, I lit it, acknowledging the evenings with Sterling Hayden aboard *Wanderer*. Having done that, we sat around the afterdeck in its flickering light and drank far into the night.

CHAPTER 13

PEARL DIVING ON TAKAROA

I KNEW WE were close to Takaroa because we could see the greenish reflection of the island's lagoon on the white clouds hovering above it 15 miles away. Shortly after, coconut treetops began to mysteriously pop up out of the horizon as if they were growing out of the water.

Three days earlier we had left Ua Pou in the Marquesas, and I decided to stop at Takaroa on our way to Tahiti to surprise Ramana and my friends and to tell them we would be returning for the pearl diving activities in two weeks. I was in for a shock. As we approached the village pier, I could hardly believe what I saw. The pearl diving season had begun and people from the neighboring islands had already arrived. The population had doubled, and there was a festive energy in the air. The quiet community of a year ago had transformed into a city of huts with palm-fronded sides and sheet metal roofs. Among the temporary structures were three Chinese stores and a ramshackle movie theater. I was to learn later that the stores offered canned goods, even ice cream, and old World War II movies were shown at the theater.

There was another surprise as we were coming alongside the pier and tying up our lines. From a group of watching Takaroans, I heard a voice yell out, "Aue! E taupoo api na Vini Vina!" (Alas, Winnie has a new hat!!) I was flattered. Apparently, Ramana and his friends remembered my promise to return.

For three days we observed the pearl divers in the lagoon and explored the new, expanded village. Besides offering canned goods and miscellaneous items, one store provided a pool table and served drinks. Beer was very popular among the divers and sold well after sunset, sometimes too well. Occasionally, a diver would drink too much and get out of hand. If so, the island's sole gendarme would simply handcuff him to a coconut tree until he sobered up. There was no jail on Takaroa.

We stayed a week and then cast off, promising Ramana that we would return within a month. Out of the pass and back on open water, I set sail and headed for Papeete.

It was exciting to make another Tahiti landfall, especially from the deck of my own schooner. We were on a broad reach with a strong trade wind on our port quarter. I was at the wheel and felt the breeze on the back of my neck as I looked ahead at the mountain ridges and Mount Orohena. This was my third visit to Tahiti, and its spell on me was as strong as ever.

As we were working our way up the northeast coast of the island, I gave Mike the wheel and went up forward to be alone. Sitting on the bowsprit with *Marie Celine's* bow wake rumbling under my feet, I looked out towards the coast and the black beaches. After a while, I began thinking of Rose.

We had been exchanging letters a number of times during the past year, and she knew I was returning. But her last letter seemed uncommitted and distant. I wondered if she would be in Papeete to meet me. If she was and we picked up where we left off, I had no idea where our relationship would go. I would have to take things one day at a time on this—that is, if she was in Tahiti at all.

It was late at night when we let go our anchor and tied our stern lines up to Papeete's waterfront wharf. We were ahead of schedule. Bates Littlehales, the *Geographic* photographer, wasn't due until March 15, giving us a few days to relax.

As I feared, Rose was not around, so I tried to track her down. After a few days, I finally was able to talk to one of her relatives who told me Rose had left Tahiti and was with her current boyfriend in Suva, Fiji. My heart sank. She hadn't even intimated in her letters there was someone else. This news put me in a tailspin.

I had been left out in the cold. It was a rejection I found hard to deal with. Fortunately, so much was going on, I was prevented from feeling too sorry for myself.

In the beginning, I had an agreement with Don, Mike and Jack that they would contribute as much as they could afford for provisions and maintenance of the schooner. But Mike and Jack had run out of money, and Don had to return to his job in Santa Barbara back in California. So they all had to leave. I was sorry to see them go. They had been a good crew and had gotten along well together. I was able to replace them with a 21-year-old American named Wright, who had been in Tahiti for a few months, and hired a cheerful Tahitian named Teitu who took over the cooking and would work as a deckhand when he could.

On March 15th, Bates Littlehales arrived, by the Teal Airlines flying boat, loaded down with cameras. I had his bunk ready for him. I also had two aqualungs and an air compressor, which *Geographic* had shipped over to me in California, that were lashed securely on the foredeck. That night I took Bates to the Bar Lea to drink beer and listen to the music. Thus was his brief introduction to Papeete's life.

The next morning, with bananas and avocados hanging from the rigging, we cast off our lines, hauled anchor and set sail for Takaroa. My plan was to stay there for two months so Bates would have ample time to shoot his underwater pictures of the divers while I worked on writing the article.

Hitii, a Takaroan pearl diver, was preparing to make his first dive of the day, one which would take him 120 feet down to the lagoon's bottom. An empty, weighted basket tied to a long length of rope had already been lowered. As he clung to the outrigger's side, he hyperventilated, taking four deep breaths. Then, holding a lead line in order to sink him effortlessly towards the bottom to conserve energy, he quietly disappeared under the surface. During his dive Ramana and I sat and waited. Finally, after a minute and a half, Hitii broke the surface and smiled. "Aue! Many shells!" He indicated he had found four of them which he had dropped into the submerged basket. He would probably make another 15 to 20 dives gathering as many as 100 shells before the day was over.

It was my first time out with the pearl shell divers. A few days ago we had arrived at Takaroa and unloaded all the diving gear and cameras. We also had filled Bates's aqualungs with air, using the compressor. Now, I was experiencing the underwater drama with Ramana as we watched Hitii work his magic.

There were often 30 outriggers anchored in the lagoon with two divers aboard each. They were towed out early in the morning by the three towboat outboards available and stayed until late afternoon. This scene would be repeated daily until the season was over in June. To conserve the pearl beds, diving was always held at a different island each year. This always assured a good yield. Pearls were sometimes found in the oyster shells. But the shell's greatest value was that they could be used to make, among other things, buttons, bracelets, earrings and knife handles.

Divers were prohibited from using breathing apparatus. Despite this, some of the Tuamotuans were able to hold their breath for as long as three minutes, allowing them to find three or four shells before coming back up to the surface for air. If a diver stayed down too long repeatedly, he eventually might suffer from what was called "taravana' which could cause brain damage.

Other dangers were the Moray eels who hid in coral caves ready to lash out and grab a diver's hand with their razor-sharp teeth. And there were sharks. Fortunately, the most common type was the smaller, non-threatening white-finned predator. But, occasionally, the more dangerous Hammerheads and Tiger sharks entered the lagoon, keeping the divers watchful.

To get the best underwater photographs. Bates had to be out early before the sand bottom got too stirred up, which made taking pictures impossible.

As for the divers' income, much of it came from the Chinese merchants who acted as middlemen, buying directly from the divers and then selling the pearl shell to dealers in Tahiti. At the beginning of the season, these merchants would give the diver a $170 advance. This money was used to pay the rent for an outrigger, if the diver didn't have one, as well as for an outboard and gas. What was left over was spent on clothes, canned food, movies and beer.

While we were there, the copra schooner *Vaitere* arrived and tied up at the wharf ahead of us. As she was the only link to the outside world, the usual crowd of Tuamotuans came out to see her. For 24 hours her cargo of flour, rice, canned goods and lumber were offloaded. Then sack after sack of pearl shell was packed into her hold until she was loaded down to her Plimsoll mark. The next day she left and *Marie Celine* was alone at the dock again.

For most of the two months we were in Takaroa, I worked on the article. With Bates off photographing and the crew usually ashore, I had a quiet cabin to myself. My goal was to have a final draft finished by the time we returned to Papeete so that Bates could bring it with him when he returned to the States. Later, *Geographic* published the article in the April 1962 issue under the title of "Twenty Fathoms Down for Mother-of-Pearl." It would be my first article published in a national magazine.

When I wasn't writing or out on the lagoon, I frequently dropped in on my old friend Ramana. Sometimes at night, with his battered up old guitar and ukulele, we'd play and sing Tuamotuan songs. Sometimes pigs would run through his house, and he would gently kick them with his feet to urge them out as we continued to sing. Other times we just talked.

Before we knew it, we had been at Takaroa for almost six weeks. I had finished the article, and Bates was done with the photography. It was time to go. So one day, bidding sad goodbyes to everyone, I backed *Marie Celine* away from the dock and set sail for Tahiti. A month later the pearl diving would end. The visiting islanders would dismantle their makeshift houses and load the pieces onto the *Vaitere* when she returned. The Chinese merchants would leave with their refrigerators, gasoline generators and pool tables. The movie house would be torn down. The pearl diving festival would end until the next year, and Takaroa would return to its quiet, carefree life.

After a short stay in Rangiroa, the Tuamotu's largest atoll, we sailed on to Tahiti and arrived at the end of May. Bates left shortly after with my article, and my crew of Wright and Teitu took a break ashore. I, too, needed to get away from the schooner and decided to rent a house outside Papeete and rest for a while. I also had some thinking to do. I was not sure whether I would take the *Marie Celine* back to California or continue west and sail around the world, trusting I could put together a good lecture tour afterwards.

And I thought about Rose.

I had been ashore for several months when I was approached by Alfred T. Poroi, the mayor of Papeete. He had seen the schooner tied up to the town waterfront and had gotten an idea. Calling me into his office, he offered me a tempting deal. He proposed that he buy 49% of the *Marie Celine,* hire me as captain and use her as a sightseeing venture. Work had already begun building an international airport in Punaauia which meant a bright future for Tahiti's tourism industry. His idea was to use the *Marie Celine* to take tourists to nearby Moorea for daily sightseeing tours.

If I decided to do this, he would use his influence in getting a permanent visa for me, a privilege only a handful of Americans enjoyed in French Oceania. Other details for a contract between us could be worked out later. He said he was leaving for Paris the following month on business, would stay for a week and then return to arrange for my permanent visa. The timing was good because, shortly after his return, my visa was due to expire.

I jumped at the chance. This gave me a plan. It was a unique opportunity to live in Tahiti and make a good income, as well. I thought it was the perfect chance to fulfill my dream of a life in the South Pacific.

I was wrong. Poroi left for Paris the next month as scheduled. But he didn't return when he said he would, leaving me with an expiring visa and an unprovisioned schooner with half a crew. Finally, I sent a frantic telegram to him. It was not answered, nor was a second one. Then my visa expired. A day later the French officials informed me I had to leave. My efforts to explain to them my plans with Poroi fell on deaf ears. I had to go but wasn't prepared.

I was forced to do something quickly. Fortunately, I ran into Herb Knoft, the German I had worked with aboard Sterling's *Wanderer*. Like me, he had returned to Papeete, and his new visa was still good for a few months. I knew him as an excellent and capable sailor. I told him what was happening and that I needed someone to take *Marie Celine* out of Tahiti. He could get his own crew and sail to Oahu where I could meet him. For his efforts, I would offer him as much money as I could afford. He agreed.

Two days later, having done all I could do and still not hearing from Poroi, I boarded the Teal flying boat. As we took off, I looked out the window as we flew over Papeete. I felt a horrible emptiness in my stomach and tears began rolling down my cheeks. I would have felt even worse had I known I would never lay eyes on Tahiti again.

PART II

CHAPTER 14

SETTLING DOWN

I WOULD HAVE never guessed that I was to stay ashore for the next 30 years and that my last days as owner of the *Marie Celine* would be like a bad dream.

I had been in Honolulu for a month when Herb and his crew arrived with the schooner and tied up to a slip I had reserved in one of the major marinas. They had had a tough passage, fighting headwinds most of the way and having constant squalls and bad weather. On their first night back, I treated them to dinner at a restaurant in Honolulu. I don't recall exactly how it happened, but during the meal I noticed that Herb was particularly sullen and preoccupied. When we had moved to the bar after dinner, he abruptly became angry and lashed out at me, accusing me of being selfish and irresponsible. But he didn't go into detail, leaving me to wonder whether his anger was coming from a resentment that I hadn't paid him enough or whether he misunderstood why I had to leave Papeete so hurriedly and not take *Marie Celine* up myself. It was a bad scene, and I was at a loss for words. Shortly afterwards, we parted ways, and I never saw or heard from Herb again.

I had been temporarily staying at a motel since I got back. But a few days after my fight with Herb, I found an apartment for rent on the beach under the shadow of Diamond Head. It was a beautiful location and the ideal place for me to gather myself together and decide what I was going to do with the *Marie Celine*. I gave up any idea of sailing around the world. A world voyage would be expensive with no guarantee that I would have a profitable lecture tour afterwards. And my experience with Mayor Poroi and being kicked out of Tahiti left a bad taste in my mouth.

So I reluctantly put her up for sale, asking $50,000. For a long time there were no takers until a businessman named Barkhorn offered me $37,500. At first I rejected his offer. But having no others for weeks, I finally gave in and agreed to sell at his price. The one consolation I had was that I knew he would take good care of *Marie Celine* and use her often.

As if an ending to a sad chapter, Poroi wrote me a scathing letter lambasting me for "breaking the contract" and running out on him. The fact was I never did sign any agreement with him. And he never told me why he had left me out in the cold by not answering my desperate telegrams. He finished his letter by stating he would do everything in his power to prevent me from ever getting a visa to French Oceania again.

In the months following the sale of the *Marie Celine*, I wrestled with thoughts of what my future might hold. At 26 years old, I had already lived a life few people experience. I had sailed around the world. I had revisited Tahiti twice, the first time when I nearly bought a coconut plantation, fell in love with a Tahitian girl and, ultimately, ended up with Sterling Hayden on his *Wanderer*. And the last time I had returned on my own schooner, sailing 4000 miles from California in order to write an article for *National Geographic* magazine.

What now? One possibility was trying to join the staff of *Geographic* as a writer and photographer. I already had a foot in the door. But I had not yet satisfied my wanderlust. I wanted to make one more trip. And for some reason the Philippines interested me. I had read an article about Manila and the islands of Mindanao and Cebu, and I had never been there.

So I decided to take that one final trip, a decision which would dramatically change the course of my life.

It was February 1961 when my flight touched down at Manila Airport. I checked into a hotel on Dewey Boulevard, which faced picturesque Manila Bay. The first few days I spent sightseeing around Manila. I wandered through the shopping area of Escolta, visited the famous old college of Santo Tomas, which had been converted into a concentration camp in World War II and, finally, toured the ancient city of Intramuros, where the Japanese defenders had desperately fought MacArthur's forces in 1945.

I used mostly taxis to travel around. But, occasionally, I took a jeepney, a vehicle which has become a symbol of the Filipino way of life. Jeepneys were World War II jeeps converted into small mini-buses. They had a 10-foot long rear area with bench seats, accommodating four people on each side. Above the open sides was a low sturdy roof on top of which an array of items could be lashed such as bicycles, bunches of bananas, pineapples and suitcases. All these jeepneys were painted with flamboyant colors and displayed flashy designs.

On my third day in Manila, I met Rene Dalogdog. Rene was a radio talk show host who was on the air nightly during the weekdays. Over lunch he asked me why I had come to the Philippines and was interested that I was an American writer and photographer. He asked me whether I'd be interested in being interviewed on his show. I said I would, and the next night I found myself sitting across from him in a broadcasting room with a microphone in my face.

During the interview I mentioned I had a friend who was an executive at the Philamlife Insurance Company in Honolulu. Rene laughed and said there was a Philamlife building right down the street in Ermita. Jokingly, we tossed around the idea of convincing the insurance company to start up an exchange program where an employee of the Manila branch could trade places with one from Honolulu for a year. Half in jest, I said I would have a talk with my friend when I got back to Hawaii.

Rene's program was popular and had many listeners. Proof of this was the number of letters I received later. One of them was a curious inquiry from a Philamlife secretary named Lana Reyes. She wanted to know more about the proposed exchange program and asked if she could meet me, leaving her office telephone number. I called her later, and we arranged to have lunch near her workplace. She told me she was bringing her sister Guia. It was an old Filipino custom to have a chaperon along when a woman was to meet a man for the first time.

I picked out a restaurant near her office, and we met at the agreed time. After introducing ourselves, the three of us sat down for lunch. I saw that Lana was an attractive 19-year-old Filipina, and I was taken by her right away. I listened intently as she told me about herself. She was the youngest of five siblings and was born on Masbate, an island south of Manila. Her father was a retired colonel in the Philippine Army and had been a guerilla during the Japanese occupation in World War II. After the war he had become mayor of Pasay City, a large suburb of Manila. Her mother was the niece of the late Senator Tomas Cabili, Secretary of National Defense for President Magsaysay, the Philippines' seventh president.

The lunch went well and was to be the first of many in the weeks to come. Her interest in my idea of an employee exchange to Honolulu was forgotten as the attraction we felt for one another quickly grew. Soon, I was introduced to her parents, sisters and brothers. It became a whirlwind romance and resulted in my proposing to her. After talking about it with her family, she agreed and we set a date to get married in April.

Now came the dreaded phone call to my parents, and right from the start they were upset by a number of things. To begin with, they didn't like the idea that Lana was seven years younger than I was. In addition, they were bothered by the fact she was Catholic and I was Episcopalian. But what I think troubled them the most, which wasn't discussed, was the fact that Lana was a Filipina. Being from an upper middle class background, I knew my parents frowned on mixed marriages. Our conversation, however, ended with me insisting that I was going through with it.

Future years would prove that some of their objections were right and would contribute to the deterioration of our marriage. But the biggest problem that no one talked about, was my drinking, a problem which would play a major role in our future as a couple.

After the wedding we flew to Hawaii for our honeymoon. The lease on my Waikiki apartment still had a few months left on it which gave us time to relax and be comfortable. It also gave us time to decide where we were ultimately going to live. Would it be in my country or hers? The logical place seemed to be hers. Lana had never been away from the Philippines. The only life she knew was there. I, on the other hand, had travelled all over the world and had become familiar with foreign countries and customs. It was simple logic that I would have an easier time adjusting to her home than she to mine.

With that decided, we went on to take advantage of our honeymoon. One of its highlights was the five-day visit of Mom and Dad. I was initially apprehensive about their first visit, knowing their reservations and worries about our marriage. I also felt they disapproved of our plans to settle in Manila. But for the most part, they enjoyed Honolulu. We took them on a tour around Oahu and treated them to Don the Beachcomber's restaurant in Waikiki with its native food and entertainment. And it was good that they got to know Lana. They were warm to her, and when they left I think they felt more comfortable about our future.

After spending two months in Honolulu, we returned to Manila and began to settle into married life. At the end of 1961, our first year together, we bought a house on a quiet residential street in Cubao, Quezon City, 10 miles from downtown Manila. The property was large with two houses and a swimming pool. We moved into one house and eventually rented out the other. The compound cost me $180,000.

A year later, Lana gave birth to our first child Elizabeth, who we named after Mother. Then our second child, Frederick Winston, was born the next April. "Ricky" was named after me. Both children were beautiful babies, combining the best of their Filipino and American parents' traits. And, later, we would have two more children, Philip January and Caroline Anne, our final child.

During this period I got a job at Channel 7, a local station owned by an American named Bob Stewart. For a year I wrote advertising copy for them and was involved in some directing of local programs. But, eventually, I found a better job as a copywriter at Ace-Compton Advertising agency located in Makati, a well-known business center near downtown Manila. Ace was one of the top agencies in the country. The company had clients such as Johnson & Johnson and Procter & Gamble. Potentially, there were excellent opportunities for me to move up the corporate ladder in the creative department, and I loved the job. On top of this, it was an easy 8-mile commute from our home in Cubao.

Life was being kind to us. We were comfortably settled in our new home and able to afford a live-in household staff consisting of a babysitter, a laundry woman, an errand boy and a driver for our two cars. Later, Lana would have a beauty parlor built in the corner of our property which she would name "The Magic Mirror." We also became founders of the Victoria School in Cubao, a grade school which became quite successful in future years.

In general, I was fitting into Filipino life and getting acquainted with Lana's parents, her two brothers and two sisters. I was learning to speak Tagalog, the Filipino dialect, and we were taking frequent trips to the provinces, and around Luzon with the family.

There was every indication that our future together had promise. What I didn't know at the time was that one of the most difficult chapters of my life was about to begin.

CHAPTER 15

THE AVENUE OF ADDICTION

I NEVER GAVE a thought to the possibility that I had a drinking problem. I had always considered alcohol a friend. Subconsciously, I may have been aware there was a problem, but my conscious mind ignored any signs which indicated there might have been something wrong.

There were those first two drunks I had on Nantucket before the world cruise. In and of themselves, these episodes seemed harmless enough, even though I had gotten miserable hangovers.

After all, I was only a 21-year-old college student having a good time. Later, on the *Yankee* trip, there had been more incidents of heavy drinking that I had conveniently forgotten. In Madang, New Guinea, I had gotten drunk with the bush pilots and plantation owners every night. As a matter of fact, I drank more than my shipmates in practically every port we had visited. These signs became more frequent with time. But my denial dismissed them as just a part of life.

In those days alcohol put a silver lining on everything I did, every adventure I had. I often think of the times with Sterling Hayden on *Wanderer*. There were so many nights when we were anchored in a quiet lagoon, drinking rum around the flickering light of a kerosene lantern, while listening to the distant surf on the reefs. Or that unforgettable time on board *Marie Celine,* in the Marquesas, when I broke out a bottle of Cutty Sark and celebrated with my crew the end of our 23-day passage from California. But now, five years later, alcohol seemed to have turned on me. I was becoming aware that it had stopped enhancing my life and, instead, it helped me cope with life. The enjoyment of drinking seemed to have disappeared, and I couldn't recapture it.

I remember weekends at home when I first started working for Ace-Compton. I would spend the afternoons relaxing in our bedroom watching TV. I had bought a small refrigerator and placed it beside my recliner. It held 15 bottles of beer. After lunch I would retire to the room for a "nap," lie comfortably on my recliner and reach for a beer without even getting up. I'd drink three or four and then fall asleep, only to wake up a few hours later half awake and grouchy.

On other occasions my brothers-in-law would drop in on weeknights, and we'd open a bottle of Tanduay rum. And sometimes Papa, my father-in-law, would drink with me and tell graphic stories about his experiences as a guerilla in the war. There was a lot of laughter during these get-togethers. But most of it coming from me was empty, and I was never able to bring back that feeling of carefreeness and confidence that alcohol had given me before. As far as our marriage was concerned, my drinking became an issue more and more as time went on.

I loved my job with Ace-Compton. In the beginning I was one of 10 copywriters in the creative department. Being driven the 8 miles to work by Gil, our driver, I'd arrive at the office at 8:30 a.m. My job was to write copy for print ads and TV commercials which would be presented to clients for proposed advertising campaigns. Some of the products I worked on were Tide detergents, Camay soap, Johnson & Johnson baby powder and GA Machineries. The procedure was simple. For instance, I'd come up with an idea for a product, write copy and present it to my copy group head. If approved, the art department would create visuals for the ad, either in print ad or storyboard form for TV. Then the whole package was presented to the account executive who would approve it and show it to the client.

After two years as a copywriter, I was promoted to copy group head and was given my own office. A year later, in 1967, I reached my highest position as associate creative director.

During vacations Lana and I went on trips with the children. Often, we'd drive the 150 miles to Baguio, a resort town in the middle of the northern mountains of Luzon. Another place we liked was Montebungkai, a beach resort 70 miles south of Manila. However, one trip we took stands out in my mind more than the others. It was when we traveled to Iligan City in Mindanao and stayed with the mayor, Camillo Cabili, a cousin of the family and son of the late Senator Cabili.

We had been there for a week when we were waiting to have breakfast one morning in his house. Camillo was a few minutes late, and when he finally did come down the stairs, he wore a grim look on his face.

"President Kennedy has been shot," he announced. We all sat around the table stunned. Camillo told us he had heard the news on the radio and that Kennedy had died in a Dallas hospital. It was literally a shot heard around the world, because later that morning we went into town and saw many Filipinos weeping openly in the streets. Since that day, I have talked with many people who say they knew exactly where they were and what they were doing when the news broke. I certainly do, despite the fact I was halfway around the world.

After living in the Philippines for a year, I was well on my way to becoming assimilated to the Filipino way of life. I lived in a native community and associated mostly with Filipinos and was naturally merging into their world. I learned to speak passable Tagalog, the national language, which sometimes led to interesting situations. Of all the Americans who lived in Manila, few spoke Tagalog, so no matter where I was, Filipinos assumed I didn't understand their conversations. Many times I would be standing in the checkout line at one of the supermarkets while those in front of me would be commenting on the fact that I was an American and how I was dressed or whether I was in the military or not. I usually smiled to myself and said nothing. But, occasionally, I would answer them in Tagalog, making them whirl their heads around in surprise.

By the time I was promoted to associate creative director for the agency in 1967, Lilli was 6 years old; Ricky, 5; Philip, 3; and Caroline, 2. Lilli was as beautiful as Ricky and Philip were handsome. And Caroline was still a delightful baby. In my mind they all had that special attractiveness only created by parents of different races. On top of this, every one of them showed unusual talent.

I remember when Ricky was just 4 years old and we took him golfing. Right from the beginning I was amazed at his natural ability to swing the club. Whenever I see the videos of Tiger Woods doing the same thing at this age, I'm reminded of those days with Ricky on the Capitol Hills golf course.

Lilli showed a natural talent for dancing, and we sent her to dancing school when she was very young. I remember taking her to the classes on our Vespa scooter with her little arms wrapped around me tightly as she rode behind.

When Philip was just 18 months old, he became a national model. At the time I had been assigned to work on the 1967 advertising campaign for Johnson & Johnson. My copy headline for the proposed print ad was "Happy Baby, Caressed with Johnson's Baby Powder." But we were having a difficult time finding a baby model. One day I half-jokingly suggested Philip to our casting director. She took me up on it, and months later Philip was appearing on posters and in newspaper and magazine ads all over the Philippines. He also starred in the TV commercial I wrote.

It was clear that Caroline growing up to be as beautiful a girl as Lilli. And right from the start she had an exceptional singing voice. I have always been disappointed she didn't follow up on this talent. I believe she would have become a successful pop singer.

They say it takes two to tango. But I don't think Lana had as much to do with the decline of our marriage as I did. My drinking was a major factor. It aggravated everything from arguments to impatience to outright anger. We quarreled more and more as time went on, resulting in verbal abuse, days without talking to each other and occasional separations, with me staying at hotels overnight.

On the job front things were no better. It was becoming increasingly difficult to handle my responsibilities because of the hangovers I would bring to work. As associate creative director it was my job to make presentations of our advertising campaigns to the agency's account executives and clients. I always did these myself and I was good at them. But more and more I began delegating these presentations to those under me while I sat at the meetings and watched. A fear of speaking in front of people started to grow. Soon this fear became almost paralyzing.

It all came to a head one day when we had a big presentation scheduled for Johnson & Johnson for our proposed 1968 advertising campaign. It was scheduled for a Monday at 10:00 a.m. in the agency's main conference room. Being such an important presentation, I had to lead it myself. I entered the room and saw more than a half dozen account executives sitting around our long, varnished conference table. Those on one side represented client and on the other were our people. Two easels were set up near the head of the table displaying the TV storyboard and print ads for our proposed advertising which I was to present to the clients.

This situation was nothing new to me. I had done it many times. But now it was different. Fear gripped my stomach, and my legs felt weak as I made my way up to the easels and began my presentation. My words sounded tentative and choked. It was as if I had a ball of cotton in my mouth. As I was announcing our copy strategy, my voice simply froze, and I stood in front of everyone in silence not knowing what to do. The whole room was quiet. You could have heard a pin drop. All the executives at the table were staring at me, some showing surprise and others embarrassment.

I don't remember how long I stood there. But then, as if in an out-of-the-body experience, I watched myself walk out of the conference room and into the hall to my office. There I wrote a letter of resignation, handed it to my secretary without a word and left the building. Having sabotaged my advertising career, I drove home and poured myself a scotch on the rocks.

After my breakdown at Ace-Compton, I spent the next year freelance writing. Despite drinking every day, I managed to hook up with the National Office of Mass Media, an agency which promoted and encouraged articles about the Philippines. A number of my articles were published in national magazines including the *Free Press,* Leon O'Ty's *Examiner* and the *Manila Times Sunday Magazine.* Sometimes I wrote under the pen name of Francisco Cabili to avoid being identified as an American writer doing politically-oriented articles. I remember one article I wrote for the *Free Press* which was a spoof on our moon landing in July of 1969. It was targeted at Manila's mayor, Antonio Villegas. I depicted Neil Armstrong and his crew as Filipinos who, after landing on the moon, looked back on earth to see all the potholes on Manila's streets. I also worked on a novel which, similar to the experiences of so many writers, ended up in the bottom drawer of my desk.

In my spare time I played golf with my brothers-in-law. Every Friday, Toti, Sim, Didi and I played at different golf courses around the area. There was even a time when we had tournaments each week, awarding the winner free drinks after the round. We'd stay at the clubs' bars until 5:00 or 6:00 before we went home. Often the drinking continued into the night at our house.

In 1968 Mom and Dad took a cruise to Southeast Asia and were able to visit us for a week. I was very happy to see them, and their visit provided a brief respite from my marital problems. Although I decided not to let them know that anything was wrong, I sensed they suspected something. But if they did, they kept it to themselves and enjoyed their stay. Dad and Papa got on well. On the other hand, Mom seemed somewhat uncomfortable but kept a stiff upper lip. The high point for them was meeting their grandchildren. On the last night, Lana and I threw a big party in their honor, and all Lana's relatives came to meet them. It was very difficult for me to see them finally go.

Late in 1968 we bought a condo in Marikina, a district 15 miles outside of Manila in the hills. Once we moved there, Lana's parents settled into our house in Cubao while we continued to rent the other. In Marikina, I drank more than ever and was drunk most of the day every day. Our marriage became a name only. Although Lana in her own way may have contributed to its demise, my alcoholism was the main reason. Yet, I still denied I had a problem. It was as if I had an automatic delete button in my head which went off every time I raised a glass to my lips.

I recall the overcast and gloomy afternoon when I decided I couldn't go on any longer. Lana was out of the house for some reason, and I went into the bedroom and packed my clothes. I told the children and Chrising, their nanny, I was going away for a few days and would be back. Then I called a taxi and, in tears, told the driver to take me to Ermita, the same area where I had first stayed before I met Lana. I checked into a cheap hotel, bought a bottle of Tanduay rum and sat in my room, hoping a separation might miraculously save the marriage.

It turned out I remained there for three months. I called my brother-in-law Toti and told him where I was and what was going on. I wanted his support as well as his willingness to be an intermediary between me and the family. Toti and I had become close friends despite the fact he was the only one in the family who had been dead set against our marriage in the beginning. Once or twice a week, he or Chrising would bring the kids to the nearby Luneta Park, and we all spent the day together. These reunions were difficult for me because they painfully brought out the guilt of not being with them. And the children kept asking me why I didn't come home. I had no satisfactory answer to give them.

During those three months, I lived in confusion and indecision. Not knowing whether the separation would work to save our marriage, it was impossible to make plans. I tried to induce answers by drinking every day and night at a nearby nightclub called Papagayo. I took contemplative walks in the park. I sat alone in my room drinking, attempting to find answers in the bottle. I'd meet the children at Luneta Park, after which I'd swear I'd return home. But after a while my resolve to give our marriage another chance would weaken. And, eventually, it was replaced by a new one, to leave the Philippines and go back to the States, at least temporarily.

One afternoon I went to a travel agent's office and inquired how much a round-trip ticket would cost to Kennedy Airport in New York City. Buying a round trip ticket was a commitment to myself that I was going to return. They told me it would cost $875.

Back in my hotel room, I opened a fresh bottle of rum. When night came, I took out my checkbook and, with shaking hands, wrote out a check for $875. Holding it up, I realized it was nearly illegible and that any bank teller would reject it. So I had another drink, waited 15 minutes and then wrote out a second check. Seeing it was just as illegible, I had another drink, waited again and then wrote out a third check, resulting in the same thing. These trial and error efforts repeated themselves countless times before I finally climbed into bed and passed out.

When I awoke in the morning, I saw that there were checks strewn all over the table and onto the floor.

CHAPTER 16

RETURNING HOME

THE CLAMOR of traffic woke me up that morning. Getting out of bed, I made my way to the window of my fourth floor hotel room and looked down on the swarm of cars and buses. It took me a second to realize it was rush hour on 47th Street and 8th Avenue. I had safely made it to the East Side and could hardly believe I was back in New York City after 10 long years.

Twenty-four hours earlier my plane had left Manila Airport. From Tokyo I had endured two interminable flights to Honolulu and Seattle in an old four-engine prop Constellation. After two hours in Seattle, I had boarded a Boeing 707 non-stop to New York. It was 11:00 p.m. when we touched down at Kennedy Airport. Then I had taken the long, expensive taxi ride to Manhattan's East Side and checked into a hotel.

Two weeks before in the Philippines, I called Mom and Dad and told them I was coming home and asked if they could pick me up when I arrived in New York. Having sold the house in Mendham, they were now living in Guilford, Connecticut, a three-hour drive away from the city. They had bought an old house on the East River outside nearby New Haven where Dad was now working as a dean of admissions for Yale University. So I called them from the hotel, and we agreed they'd drive down, and we'd meet in the lobby that afternoon.

Our meeting proved quite emotional for them, something I had rarely seen. They hugged me tightly and then stepped back and gave me concerned looks. Gaunt and pale, I resembled a shaggy apparition. Stressed out and exhausted from the past year's marital problems and excessive drinking, I had lost a lot of weight and was less than 120 pounds. Helping me with my luggage, Mom and Dad walked with me to the car, and we started the drive back to Guilford. Within an hour we were out of the city's noise and on the Merritt Parkway, winding through the quiet woods of Connecticut.

Towards evening we pulled into the driveway of their new home. It was a beautiful old house built in 1793 and nestled along the banks of the East River. To one side was an old red barn with Mom's new flower garden on the other. After I got settled in an upstairs bedroom, we talked in the living room until late in the evening. During the conversation they naturally asked me how long I planned to stay before returning to the Philippines. I had no answer. I thought it might be a month, maybe two. Or, perhaps, I would not go back at all. I hadn't decided. We did agree I would remain with them for the time being.

So I stayed in Guilford for a few months, giving myself a chance to regain my emotional and physical strength before I made a decision that I apprehensively knew I'd have to make.

A few days after I had arrived, Mom and Dad asked if I had ever thought of seeing a doctor. To them I looked like a train wreck, and it was obvious I had been drinking too much for too long.

Doctor Adams thought so, too. Taking my parents' advice, I had made an appointment to see her a week later. She was Guilford's most popular doctor and was well respected. She took one look at me and told me I had better cut down on my drinking, better yet, stop. After checking me over thoroughly, she asked if I would like to talk to the former town drunk who had been sober for the last eight years. I said I would. She called him and he was there in 15 minutes. I sat with him in an empty side office where he told me his story—how miserable his life had been drinking and how he had stopped. I listened quietly while he talked but convinced myself I was not as bad off as he had been.

But I did follow Doctor Adams's strong suggestion to cut down on the drinking and decided I would go "on the wagon" for a while. The result was I didn't have a drink for the next six months. And because of my abstinence, I gained weight, slept better and began to get my color back.

But depression and worry persisted, caused by an almost intolerable indecision, should I return to the Philippines and my family or not? When I thought of not going back, the guilt of abandoning my children and ignoring my responsibilities as a father was painful. But there was the other side of the coin, too. It was important that I take care of myself rather than to return to a marriage I was unable to cope with and in which I was miserably unhappy. What kind of atmosphere would that make for the children, with Lana and I fighting all the time?

Then the day came when I made the decision. I just reached the point when I knew I wasn't going back. Although this choice filled me with shame, I felt relief at the same time. I sat down and wrote Lana a letter telling her I was getting a divorce and promising to regularly send money for the children. When I mailed it, I knew I was not only giving up the children but also considerable property investments we had made in the Philippines.

For better or worse, I was moving on with my life.

My parents had been more than helpful allowing me to stay with them. But after six months I decided to rent an apartment in Hartford. At 34 years old, I needed to be on my own.

I chose Hartford for two reasons. The first was that I had gone to Trinity College there, and it was familiar ground. The second was I would be near Donnie who lived in West Hartford with his first wife, Lucia, and worked in the city. While I had been in the Philippines, he had attended the University of Virginia Law School, passed the bar and had eventually become a partner in a law firm located in downtown Hartford.

Consequently, I settled into a one-bedroom apartment on Washington Street, a few blocks from the Capitol building. Once settled, I sat down and regrouped my life. I considered myself lucky. I still had a monthly income from my trust, a car which Mom and Dad had generously bought for me and sufficient furniture. Now, I could see my brother anytime I wanted. And I had the opportunity to pick up my writing again and to work on an article I had in mind about Guilford for *Connecticut Magazine*.

On the other hand, although lessened somewhat, my depression and guilt feelings still persisted. This provided a good excuse to pick up drinking again. Having abstained for six months, I felt this was proof enough I really didn't have that much of a problem with alcohol. Just to be sure, this time I would control my drinking. To do this, I decided not to have my first drink until evening time when the news came on at 6:00. After that there would be no rules. I could drink as much as I wanted until I went to bed.

Unfortunately, this plan was flawed. The fact was that, while doing this, I was actually mentally drinking all day. That is, in the mornings, my mind was counting the hours to 6:00 when

I could have a drink. This mental countdown happened every day. 6:00 in the evening became the most important time of the day. When that magical hour of the day came, I settled down and drank one drink after another until I went to bed sloshed. So this plan didn't last very long, and soon I was back to my old ways. I had never heard the truism that "if you have to control, you're out of control."

My brother being near was a Godsend. My visits to West Hartford, however, were sometimes uncomfortable because of the presence of his wife, Lucia. In her eyes I was a rebel who had refused to conform to the social lifestyle she approved of. So, for much of the time, Donnie and I met for lunch in a restaurant near his downtown office.

Another Godsend was a rebirth of my interest in birdwatching and what it led to. One day after I had lived in Hartford for a while, on a whim I bought a pair of binoculars and a Peterson's field guide. Then I took a drive down to Old Saybrook on the coast to check out shore birds. This day turned out to be therapeutic. While looking for Oystercatchers, Great Blue Herons and Least Sandpipers, I felt a sense of well-being and serenity I hadn't experienced in years. Birding was helping me live in the moment.

Shortly thereafter, I met someone who would have an enormous positive influence on my life. I was birding in Reservoir #6 outside West Hartford in May of 1972. The area happened to be thick with warblers, my favorite species, particularly Black-throated Greens and Blackburnians. Doing much of my field work by identifying bird songs, I was driving slowly along the forest edge with the car window down and listening. Then I noticed someone ahead who was looking through a pair of binoculars. Obviously, he was a birdwatcher, too, so I quietly coasted up beside him and asked what he was seeing. Without looking up, he answered he "had" a Black-throated Blue. Then he glanced up and asked if I was a birder, too. I told him I was and that I had just heard a Chestnutsided Warbler in the dogwood tree across the road. Getting out of the car, I walked up to him and introduced myself.

His name was Paul Carrier, and he was a 28-year-old freelance artist and passionate ornithologist. We ended up talking for a long time and quickly felt a strong connection with one another. As a matter of fact, it was one of those rare times when you meet someone who you feel you've known forever—a soul mate experience, if you will.

When I finally left to go home, we agreed to meet later in the week and spend a day birding together. And we did. What we discovered that day was that we made the perfect birdwatching team. Paul had extraordinarily sharp eyes, and I was good at bird song identification. From that time on, we would meet three or four times a week for the next two years. In the process we would become best friends.

There were good benefits resulting from my meeting with Paul. One was that I got back to my love of birdwatching. This helped me temporarily forget about the guilt of being 7000 miles away from my children. And our friendship at least put a brake on my daily drinking. For one thing, I couldn't carry a bottle of scotch in my hip pocket while we were walking in the woods. And in the beginning I didn't want him to know I drank as much as I did. This might have been one of my first subconscious admissions that my drinking habits made me different from others. A final benefit was meeting Paul's family. His brother, Doug, lived in Simsbury with his wife and two children, and we often spent time there. It wasn't long before I began feeling like a part of the family. This lessened my depression significantly.

Paul introduced me to something I had never before experienced while birdwatching in the past. That was the world of hawks. Each September along the New England coast and the inland mountain ranges, the broad-winged hawks migrate south to Central America for the winter. They sometimes flew in huge flocks, called "kettles," and hawk watchers gathered at strategic points on hilltops and shore points to watch this parade of raptors.

These hawk migrations are one of the most fascinating phenomena of nature. When the first cold fronts move through in mid-September, large numbers of broad-wings group up early in the morning in the deciduous treetops lining the valleys. When the sun warms the land and the first thermals begin, these groups take to the air, slowly spiraling upwards thousands of feet. In some groups there are as many as 500 hawks. Gaining altitude, they form a thick kettle which resembles a whirlwind of distant leaves swirling in slow motion towards the clouds. When the leading hawk gets high enough, he peels off and those behind, one by one, follow him. Soon there is a line of "stooping" birds gliding in single file southwards for miles until they lose altitude and are forced to kettle up again. It is at this stooping stage when they are most easily counted by hawk watchers. During ideal weather conditions, when the wind is in the right direction and the thermals are strong, it's possible to sometimes see over 3000 broad-wings in one day.

Hawk watch teams and locations were almost non-existent in Connecticut in 1972. Paul and I were one of the first to organize one which met on top of the 500-foot hill across the road from his brother's house. Today, the watches are well organized and spread all over the state where often there will be 15 to 20 people on the same hill. Now, the daily number of hawks at any one of the hawk watch locations is reported to the Audubon Society and published in local bird club newsletters.

Our main preoccupation, however, was the warblers. More than a dozen species of these beautiful birds would arrive during spring migrations in May. One time I remember watching six different kinds of these birds in one tree. The most exciting occurrence was when Paul and I established a record.

One day when Paul had to work, I was alone walking along Powder Mill Road, a dirt back lane near Collinsville. It ran along a ravine with the Farmington River on one side and a steep wooded hill on the other. At some point I heard a warbler singing - a song which was unfamiliar to me. The bird was above the road high in the trees covering the ridge's slope. All I could see was a silhouette fluttering from one branch to another. After a quarter of an hour's neck stretching, I gave up. I called Paul that night and told him that the bird might have been a Cerulean Warbler.

The next day both of us went back and, within 5 minutes, Paul's sharp eyes proved I was right. Every day for a week we returned to find him still there. Then we spotted his mate and eventually found their nest. We now knew we were seeing the first pair of breeding Ceruleans ever seen east of the Appalachian Range. Subsequently, we notified the Hartford Bird Club, and the word got out quickly. Three days later I was surprised to see a line of parked cars along Powder Hill Road with license plates from New York State, Rhode Island, Maine and Massachusetts. Three months later, our find was published in the Audubon Society's trade magazine in which we were given full credit for setting an ornithological record.

When I wasn't birding with Paul, I was working on an article for *Connecticut Magazine* about the town of Guilford. To research this, I had to make several trips down to Mom and Dad's, sometimes spending the night. I shot photographs and read up on the town's history using its library. One trivial fact I included in the article was the location of a stone monument on the green in Guilford center. It had a bronze plaque on which was inscribed: "At this spot on Thursday, 1754, absolutely nothing happened."

Visits with my parents were usually pleasant. Now in his 70's, Dad had retired from his job as a dean of admissions for Yale and was now doing volunteer work a few days a week at a home for the retarded in New Haven. He still retained his wonderful enthusiasm for life which I had always admired. As far as Mom was concerned, I continued to overlook all the things she had done for me, like paying for the *Yankee* world cruise years ago and, more recently, buying me a car to have in Hartford. Instead, I focused on her obvious disapproval of my life choices in general. She often asked what I planned to do in the future besides writing. And I know she was quietly aware and critical of my heavy drinking.

I finished the Guilford article which was published a few months later in *Connecticut Magazine*. In my spare time I visited Donnie and Lucia in their West Hartford home, and Donnie and I alone often enjoyed lunch together at a restaurant near his office. Lucia had already given birth to their first child, Rowe. Later a daughter, Merrill, and a son, Brad, would follow.

In early 1973, I was introduced to marijuana to which I quickly became addicted. Paul and I had been to a party with some friends of his and, during the course of the evening, someone passed a bong around. This first time I took weed didn't have much effect on me. But after being on it a few weeks, I was getting stoned just like everyone else. When I was on this drug, it was easy for people to "play with my head" and convince me of ridiculous things, such as the fact I didn't exist or that the cops were after me. What I remember most were the ping pong games I played while stoned. Repeatedly, I would swing and completely miss the ball. When I finally was able to slam it, it seemed to float slowly across the net and take forever to reach my opponent's side. Paul seldom participated in these drinking and smoking sprees. But it was obvious that he had become aware of my heavy involvement and my denial that anything was wrong.

During the spring of the same year, and after the warbler migrations had ended, I decided to take a trip to Nantucket and spend a few days at our old summer home on North Liberty Street. It had been 15 years since I'd last been there.

I should have known what would happen. I fell back in love with the island. Driving to Torn Nevers Head, like I used to, I re-experienced the magnetic view of the blue Atlantic Ocean. I saw the familiar old mansions on Main Street again, and I took in the island's tranquility and slow pace.

On my return to Connecticut, I was asking myself why I was living in the commotion of downtown Hartford. I thought of all the wonderful memories I had of the island and how happy I'd been there. Why couldn't I just move there? The price I would have to pay was leaving my brother and Paul. But I could always visit them.

By the time I arrived back at my Washington Street apartment, I had already made up my mind.

CHAPTER 17

THE 23 STEPS

MY NEW home was a small, second-floor studio apartment with a 23-step flight of outside stairs leading up to a landing and a front door. Nestled on New Lane, a quiet street on the outskirts of Nantucket town, it had a combination bedroom/kitchen connected by a short hallway to a living room. There was a nice view, from my windows of the Unitarian Church's gold dome, and the rent was just $175 a month.

It was July and I had left Hartford in my Volkswagen beetle packed with everything I owned. I was looking forward to living year around on the island that held so many good memories of the past. I would have been even happier if I had known I was in for some exceptional luck which would give my intermittent career as a writer an enormous boost.

Shortly after I had settled in, I was surfcasting one day at the Jetties beach near the channel entrance. I noticed the man fishing next to me had a striking resemblance to James Cagney, the Hollywood actor. As a matter of fact, at first I thought it was James Cagney. Curious, I went over and introduced myself. His name was Bill Daly. We chatted for a while until he asked me what I did. I told him I was a writer and photographer. This seemed to stir his curiosity. He turned and pointed to his wife, Joe Ann, who was lying on the beach behind us and told me she was an editor for the publisher Dodd, Mead in New York. Inviting me to come up with him, he introduced her to me.

As we talked, I quickly became aware she was interested that I was a writer and that I lived on Nantucket. She said Dodd, Mead wanted to do a book about the island and its whaling history and they were looking for a writer and photographer to take on the project. Twenty minutes later, she asked me if she could see some samples of my writing. Excited at this turn of events, I invited both of them to my place for drinks that night.

When they arrived that evening, we sat down in my small living room. While Bill and I had drinks, Joe Ann read some tear sheets of my articles. After a time she looked up and said she liked my style and asked whether she could bring the samples and some of my photographs back with her to show the editorial board. I said "yes," hardly able to contain my excitement.

After they left, a month went by and then she called. She said the board liked what they saw and wanted to contract me to do a book. What they were looking for was a capsule history of the island, highlighting the whaling era and supported by my photographs. Joe Ann told me they were willing to advance me $2000 to start the project. She'd send a contract out for me to sign in a week. Good to her word, it was in my mail 10 days later.

I don't remember if there was a deadline, but I started working on a manuscript immediately. We agreed I would write one chapter at a time. I would send it in, she'd edit it and then send it back to finalize. When not working on the manuscript, I was out shooting pictures - when the weather was good.

Looking back, it seems like a miracle that I did some of my best and managed, at the same time, to continue my drinking. I would have never guessed that my book would sell well and even draw favorable reviews in the *New York Times* and the *Boston Globe*.

My drinking determined my daily schedule. It was part of the whole process. I'd sit down to write around 11:00 in the morning when my hangover from the previous night had eased enough. Working until mid-afternoon, I'd stop for the day, go out and take pictures, if I had to, and then return to my recliner in front of the TV set and break open my first beer. I would then drink steadily until 9:00 or 10:00 at night and then go to bed in a half-stupor.

Waking up the next morning with a hangover, I'd wait until 11:00 or noontime before I was able to write again. Thus it would go, day after day.

I had difficulty shooting pictures. It was the old problem of my shaking hands, and the results were blurred photographs. This forced me to set my shutter speed at 1/500th of a second instead of 1/60th for standard shots.

With Joe Ann frequently calling and sending back suggested edits for each chapter, I finally managed to finish the book in 10 months. Sending it in, I impatiently waited. In the spring of 1975, I got the phone call. Joe Ann told me that the editorial board was pleased and had decided to send the book to the printers as soon as they could. And they had approved of my title, *Nantucket Then and Now*. The time of publication, they said, would be in late 1976 or early 1977.

Now, with celebrating as an excuse, my alcohol consumption took off. By spring I was drinking non-stop, beginning as soon as I got out of bed in the mornings. By afternoon I would take a "nap," wake up a few hours later and continue to drink until I went to bed. Most of the time I spent at home, but occasionally I went out. I had friends who smoked pot and hash, and I would get stoned with them. Combined with alcohol, these drugs did a number on me. As during my days in Hartford, people took advantage of my gullibility, convincing me of a number of strange things like having a different name. And several times on my way home after a pot and wine party, I'd swear I had passed Nantucket's historic Old Mill twice.

When I look back, drinking led to things I now consider amusing, but at the time were not. One incident, of all things, concerned my trash. I was routinely drinking Napa Sonoma wine out of gallon bottles and putting the empties in my trash bags. When the bags were full, I'd take them out to the town dump in Madaket. In those days there weren't any recycling centers, so everyone would go to the dump and throw their trash into a deep pit. Whenever I threw mine, there would always be the resounding smash of breaking glass, and those nearby would curiously stare at me.

There was one incident that should have told me my mind was going strange. I was alone at home drinking wine and smoking pot when suddenly I had a kind of ethereal awakening. It was in the form of a thought that repeated itself over and over again revealing to me *The Answer* to life. Struggling out of my recliner, I went to my desk and wrote it down on a pad lying on the desk. The next morning, hungover with eyes half open, I remembered I had had some kind of revelation the night before and had written it down. Thinking I had found the answer to everything and that now I was to experience bliss for the rest of my life, I made my way into the living room to the pad on my desk. But my heart sank when I read what I had scrawled: "The grass is green."

Alcohol, too, failed to relieve a constant sense of guilt about leaving my children. My communication with them was ongoing, and some of their letters contained snapshots. Looking at these was heart wrenching. At that time Lilli was 12; the boys, 11 and 8; and Caroline, 7. Seeing them grow up filled me with remorse. All I was capable of doing was to reply, writing that I loved them and that sometime soon we'd be together again.

Ironically, while constantly drinking, I made attempts to grow in my spiritual life. I studied the New Age philosophies, poured through books about Zen and Buddhism and read articles written by Ram Dass in the *New Age Journal*. But anything I might have learned was quickly drowned and forgotten by my drinking.

One saving grace during this period was my friendship with Rollin Manville, a childhood friend I met on the Wauwinet beach when we were both 10 years old. Sometimes I would stop drinking long enough to go fishing with him, and we would have long talks. This had a stabilizing effect. Rollin had a job as a caretaker for a house out in Polpis outside of town. It was owned by Felix Pappalardi, the lead musician and producer for the rock groups Cream and Mountain, the latter known particularly for its signature songs "Mississippi Queen" and "Nantucket Sleighride." Often, "Fi," as we called him, invited Rollin and me out to his house to party. We'd sit in his living room and listen to him play various rock hits. I fit right in with my long hair as I smoked pot and assumed a "hip" attitude. I could have passed for a Woodstock graduate.

Soon after Dodd, Mead had accepted my manuscript in 1975, Mom and Dad decided to move to Nantucket and live there year round. It was principally Dad who wanted to make the move. Mom was less enthusiastic because she loved Guilford, and she would also have to give up her garden which equaled the beauty of her Mendham one from years ago. As a matter of fact, it was so impressive that the Guilford Garden Club had it on its regular scheduled tour.

I had mixed emotions about their coming to Nantucket. Naturally, I didn't want them to see how much I was drinking, although they probably guessed by now. Also, I thought about our old North Liberty Street house right down the street being so near my tiny walkup apartment. It made me uncomfortable and I'm sure made Mom uncomfortable, too. I could imagine her friends at the Garden Club, where she would become president in later years, wanting to ask why her 38-year-old son was renting a studio apartment instead of owning a home like hers and enjoying a job with a six-figure salary.

Once they had moved in, I saw them on a regular basis. I must have looked like a mess with my long, hippy style hair and my thin, haggard appearance. I'm sure they couldn't help but see the emptiness and unease in my face. It didn't occur to me at the time that they were ashamed of my appearance and worried about my health. So wrapped up in myself, I was completely unaware of what I was putting them through.

After my book had gone to the printers in the summer of 1976, drinking became my total world. If I needed an excuse, it would have been that I was rewarding myself now that I was becoming a published author. My life continued to slide downhill very quickly.

I began to have blackouts. Some mornings upon awakening, I'd look out the window to make sure my Volkswagen Beetle was there. Sometimes at parties, I got so drunk that I had to be driven home in someone else's car. If the telephone rang, I was afraid to answer it, fearing I'd slur my words. I stopped having breakfast at the Dory, a small coffee place on India Street, because my hands shook, so I was spilling coffee on the counter all the time. I started feeling that I was losing control of my life, yet, insisted I wasn't.

The most painful thing was the deterioration of my emotional state. My depression kept getting worse. The enthusiasm I had always had for life, which I had inherited from Dad, was slipping away. For instance, I had loved fishing all my life and looked forward to the times when Rollin and I would take his boat out to Great Point and troll for bluefish. But I didn't go anymore. When I drove out to my old favorite spot at Tom Nevers Head, the blue Atlantic didn't lift my spirits the way it used to. The most important thing to me now was the next drink. Having an empty refrigerator with no beer was frightening. Which one of the town's three liquor stores would I go to each day, fearing if I went to only one, the owner would see how much booze I was buying. By October I was a recluse. My world became my little apartment and a bottle of beer or wine.

One night in late October, I managed to get out and go over to Rollin's place where I got very drunk. I don't know how I drove home without having an accident. I recall struggling out of the car and slowly making my way to the foot of the apartment stairs. I stopped and looked up the 23 steps and wondered whether I could make it. My front door way up at the top might as well have been the summit of Mount Everest.

The next thing I became conscious of was sitting on my living room floor with a bottle of wine and a pipe full of pot. I was sobbing uncontrollably with tears running down my face. At that moment I realized that I was a prisoner to alcohol. Complete defeat consumed me, and I began to see what drinking had taken away from me in the last 10 years. I had lost a wife and four children, a four-bedroom home in Manila and substantial property I had invested in, in the Philippines. I had lost a career in advertising as a creative director. I no longer had a nice Mercedes Benz and a private parking space at Ace-Compton with my name on it. The Mercedes had now been replaced by a 1968 Volkswagen Beetle with 200,000 miles on it, a plastic flower on the tip of its radio aerial and a bumper sticker which read "I Love Janis Joplin." And I had wasted away my inheritance money. I was a total failure at 40 years old.

Perhaps the worst thing of all was that I had lost myself. I didn't know who I was or where I wanted to go. I was weighed down with depression, guilt and self-centered fear. Alcohol and pot had beaten me. I only know one thing: I didn't want to live the way I was living any longer. I had had enough. I could go no further.

At 4:00 in the morning I called Rollin.

CHAPTER 18

REVIVAL

"Why the hell are you drinking so much?" Rollin asked as he poured a cup of tea for me in his kitchen. "You think you're one of those people who can't handle it?"

I nodded my head silently. Without saying a word, it was the first time I had confessed to anyone, let alone myself, that I might have a problem with alcohol. This admission brought instant relief that quieted down the remorse and sense of defeat within me.

We talked for a long time. I knew what I had to do. It was obvious I needed to be detoxed. So Rollin drove me to the Nantucket

Cottage Hospital where I admitted myself. They put me in a room alone on the second floor, hooked me up intravenously and let me sleep. I didn't wake up until late afternoon when I was aware that a doctor was standing at my bedside. Giving me a cursory examination, he told me I was being treated for acute alcoholism and they had decided to keep me in the hospital for several days.

That night Herb Stevens, the Episcopal minister, a friend of my parents, visited me. He had been making his usual rounds at the hospital and hadn't known I was there. I talked for a while as he listened quietly. I don't remember our conversation specifically. I do recall him warning me that it was going to be a difficult road to sobriety, but that he'd help me in any way he could. He mentioned there was a recovery program on the island that I could, perhaps, look into. When he left, I fell asleep again, completely forgetting I hadn't even told Mom and Dad I was in the hospital.

The next day I felt a little better, but my mind was full of thoughts about what life would be like without drinking. The prospect made me apprehensive. Would I even have the willpower to stay sober?

Then in the afternoon a couple walked into my room who I had never seen before. Their names were Mickey and Sue. Mickey was an attorney and Sue, a taxi driver. They told me they were members of the recovery program in town and that Herb Stevens had told them I was in the hospital. They sat down at the foot of my bed, and I listened to what they had to say.

Each shared about their days as active alcoholics, the suffering and misery they had gone through because of it and how they were able to get sober. They described what they had lost in their lives, the depression and guilt they experienced and hopelessness they had lived with. They explained how they had found the program for alcoholics which had helped them to stop drinking. Mickey confided he had been sober 19 years and Sue, 12. Because of the recovery program their lives had become infinitely better. For the first time in years, they had felt truly happy and at peace with life. They had changed. Their self-centeredness had lessened. Their fear and anxiety had been replaced by peace of mind. They had learned to accept life on life's terms. And they had gotten back most of the material things they had lost. When they finally left, Sue handed a book to me which she referred to as "The Big Book." She told me I could have it and that there might be some things in it which could help me.

After they had gone, I thought about everything they had said, as I held the book in my hands. Then I opened it and read the first paragraph I saw. It was on page 152, and it alluded to becoming sober. It read "…you will find release from care, boredom and worry. Your imagination will be fired. Life will mean something at last. The most satisfactory years of your life lay ahead."

These words hit me like a bombshell. I paused and listened to the sounds floating through my room's open window. They were the distant cheers of spectators at a football game going on across the street on Nantucket High School's playing field. I realized that I wanted to be a part of those sounds—to be a part of living normally again and doing what normal people do rather than sit in my recliner all day getting drunk. This thought, added to what I had just read, changed something inside me. It was as if a light bulb had been turned on in my head, and I began to feel calm. With it grew a genuine sense of hope, something I had not felt for so long.

I didn't realize that at this minute I was experiencing a psychic change and a huge turning point in my life. It was Friday, October 29, 1976, a day I will never forget. I couldn't have known that for the next 35 years I would never pick up a drink again.

During my first year of sobriety, my life slowly began to turn around. I went to meetings every night. Some were held in people's homes, others at the Catholic and Episcopalian churches. Miraculously, my physical cravings for alcohol stopped almost immediately. I met new and supportive friends. I started to learn the many tools of the program that helped me not only to stay sober but to grow as a person. After three months, I was introduced to service and was asked to make the coffee every week at the meeting in St. Mary's Catholic church. My coping skills grew back, and my priorities changed drastically as my self-centeredness lessened. My old enthusiasm for life returned as did my sense of humor. I loved the program and what it was doing for me.

But there were life's usual bumps that first year, too, and my sobriety was tested. Charlie Burke, who had been the family's financial advisor for years, called me. He informed me there was only $5000 left in my trust fund and suggested I cash in the amount. This was a huge financial blow which was only softened by the fact that my book was coming out in March. As luck would have it, Herb offered me the job of sextant at the Episcopal church.

I know that Mom and Dad were tremendously relieved I wasn't drinking anymore. But Mom must have cringed to see her Groton graduate son become the janitor of the very church she attended. Yet, this menial job kept me financially alive and was good for my mental health, as well.

As scheduled, *Nantucket Then and Now* came out in March. Shortly after, I was sitting at a table near the entrance of Mitchell's bookstore with two piles of my books in front of me, signing copies for people who were standing in line. And, to my surprise, excellent reviews had come in. The *New York Times* had written, "What's most remarkable about Nantucket, as clear photos of landmark houses and churches and lighthouses point out, is that 'Now' isn't so very different from 'Then.' In a brisk tour of the island, Williams proves to be a genial guide." The *Boston Globe* commented, "This is a welcome addition to our volumes of New England lore…the book offers information and enjoyment for everyone…"

But my money situation forced me to look for a better job. My sextant's position was paying a minimum salary, and my writing income promised to be sporadic as with most freelance writers. I needed something steadier that paid well. Since I was involved with addiction recovery, I looked into the counseling field.

Nantucket had no rehab or detox centers, so I had to consider the Cape Cod area 30 miles away on the mainland. After spending a week there, I found a position with the Pocasset Detox. The job was funded by the government and lasted just a year. But I took it.

Nine months had gone by since I admitted myself into the Nantucket Cottage Hospital. Now, in the summer of 1977, I found myself moving again for the sixth time in my adult life. Some might say I was looking for a "geographic" cure, while others would claim I was just experiencing life's randomness. It was probably a little bit of both. Eventually, I found another second-floor apartment (this time with interior stairs), in Centerville, 6 miles west of Hyannis. I returned to the island and said goodbye to Mom and Dad, Rollin, some old friends and Nantucket Island.

With almost a year of sobriety under my belt, I was definitely realizing that life was worth living despite the ups and downs that might await me in the future.

CHAPTER 19

CAPE COD

I HAD ALWAYS loved Cape Cod, and it was a place which had continued to grow on me over the years. Maybe it was because there were a lot of similarities to Nantucket, like the rolling moors, the endless Atlantic beaches and the traditional Cape Cod style houses with their white picket fences. I had visited here many times before , and there was a familiarity about it that made settling into my new home in Centerville an easy move.

And I looked forward to my new job. If someone were to tell me that in the next 10 years I would have seven of them in five different fields, I wouldn't have believed them. Like Ace-Compton, my alcoholism counselor's position was to be a steady paycheck-to-paycheck job, something I sorely needed.

Located some 15 miles west of Centerville, Pocasset was a typical Cape town with a general store, a post office and a small boatyard. Surrounding the town were beautiful clapboard-sided vacation homes with shingled roofs. The detox was located just outside the town's center at the small local hospital. A separate three-story building on the complex housed the detox on the first floor and a "half-way" house on the top two floors. The house was called *Penthouse 1* and offered a 28-day program for those addicts who had ended their detoxification. Both floors had rooms with beds accommodating 20 men. There was also a meeting room.

It was here where I, and three other counselors, worked. Generally, I was busy with one-on-one sessions with the residents. It was true that I had no counseling experience, but I was a pro in knowing what active alcoholism does to a person's life. This helped me identify with them and understand their fears and sense of hopelessness. When I was on the night shift, I would drive six to eight residents to a program meeting nearby in an old 1972 Volkswagen van. And, occasionally, I led the regular meetings where the 12 steps of recovery were taught.

Often the job was frustrating. Some residents would stay for the entire 28 days and then go out and drink again. Of these, a few returned to detox weeks or months later. One individual had 120 admissions to detox in 10 years. But there were others who never came back, either denying they had a problem or dying to prove they did. Alcoholism is a baffling disease. And all too often it's fatal.

As far as my own sobriety was concerned, it was strengthened by the job. I had the chance to see what addicts go through during their first days of recovery. In the process my own recovery was reinforced. And to strengthen it even more, I went to many recovery meetings around the Cape when I wasn't working. All this involvement was helping me grow as a person. I found myself becoming more confident, yet less self-centered. I was more honest with others, as well as with myself. And the hope I had first felt in the hospital a year ago was even stronger.

I learned that one of the keys to good sobriety was to help others. In recovery there were countless ways of doing this. One of them was by speaking. The first time I experienced this was one night in front of 200 people, at a podium on a stage in Brockton outside of Boston.

To describe this night, I have to go back to Ace-Compton days in the Philippines when I was making presentations and had choked up with fear at that important Johnson & Johnson meeting. Ever since, the anxiety of speaking in front of an audience had continued to plague me. So for the first two years in the program, I had turned down any requests to talk in front of groups. But, eventually, I could no longer avoid it. One day the secretary of a group informed me I had been scheduled to speak at a big meeting in Brockton.

When the day came, my anxiety was so overwhelming that I was sick and had to call Pocasset and tell them I wasn't coming in. Then, for the rest of the day, I paced up and down in my living room trying to keep my mind off things by watching TV. But as the day went on, my apprehension grew. By 6:00 that evening, when two others from the recovery group picked me up, I was a nervous wreck. We drove the 40 miles to Brockton and pulled up to the meeting hall. When we entered I saw a crowd of people milling around. On the stage was a menacing podium which seemed to be mocking me.

The meeting began with a brief opening format after which I was introduced. I hardly remember walking up onto the stage and to the podium. But I clearly recall the moment when I turned towards the audience and saw the mass of faces staring up at me.

Then something unreal happened. As I started to speak, I felt myself begin to float above my left shoulder. It was like I was a spectator looking down at myself. I watched and listened to myself make the opening remarks. At the same time, all my fear and anxiety suddenly vanished and was replaced by a sense of peace I had never experienced before. And with it was a new confidence and the knowledge that I could do anything I wanted. I was unaware of how long the suspension lasted. But, gradually, I settled back into my body and went on with the speech for the next 20 minutes as if I had been doing it all my life.

What I didn't understand that night was that I had had an out-of-body experience, known today as an OBE. For many back in those days of the '70's, OBEs were considered paranormal hocus-pocus. And the few who believed in them were hesitant to say anything to avoid ridicule. But since then thousands of OBEs around the world have been verified, indicating mine was not that unusual. After years of research, well-known cardiologists like Drs. Pin van Lommel and Jeffery Long have validated the reality of the OBE. And they have discovered that the OBE is not only caused by the body stress of patients in surgery, but also by extreme mental and emotional tension, which I certainly was dealing with in Brockton. The result of this incident changed me in some way. After that night, and to this day, I have had much more curiosity about the paranormal, psychic experiences and spiritual growth.

I have never forgotten that Brockton experience.

My year's term as counselor at *Penthouse 1* ended in 1978, and I began looking for another job. I found one almost immediately. My old friend and *Yankee* shipmate Ed Crosby lived in the next town of Osterville. His family had owned Chester A. Crosby & Sons boatyard for generations. I was visiting Ed and Jeannie, his wife, one day when he asked me if I wanted to work at the yard. I said I would and started the very next week. The benefits were obvious. Not only was I back on a payroll, but I also lived in Centerville, only three miles to the west. Most of all, I was returning to the world of boats and water after almost 20 years. It was not going back to sea again, a yearning which had never left me, but it would do. I worked as an assistant rigger for the next two years and a store clerk for a third year. My paycheck of $200 a week got me by, and the physical work was good for me.

Often I had chances to see Ed. Unfortunately, because of his ill health, he didn't come to his office every day. The diabetes he had suffered from, on the world cruise and which ultimately forced him to leave *Yankee* in Suva, had worsened over the years. Shortly after I started working at the yard, his condition began to deteriorate rapidly, and he steadily weakened and lost weight. By the time I had been transferred to the marine store, Ed had been taken to the hospital in Boston twice. We rarely saw him at his office and when we did, he looked gaunt.

One Sunday in 1981, Ed and Jeannie invited me for supper at their house. It turned out to be a special evening. Jeannie cooked a delicious meal and afterwards, around the table, she listened to Ed and me reminisce. The two of us talked about our experiences together during the *Yankee's* summer cruises and shared the happy times we had had in the South Pacific. It was a night when I felt closer to him than I ever had before.

The following morning I arrived at work, as usual, and was told that Ed had been flown to the Doctors' Hospital in Boston an hour after I left to go home the night before. He had started hemorrhaging. Jeannie called 911, and he was transported by helicopter. The yard was unusually quiet the whole day and into Tuesday. On Wednesday morning Ed passed away, leaving us all in shock.

Hearing the news was a shock, and I just stood for a while trying to absorb it. Then, instinctively, I went out the front entrance of the yard to the flagpole and lowered the flag to half-mast. I was thinking how thankful I was that Ed and I had had dinner together with Jeannie just a few nights ago. Ed's passing was a loss for the entire Osterville community. This was underscored by the turnout at his funeral. There was a procession of at least 30 cars and limos stretching out for a quarter of a mile.

It was 1981, and I had been working at Crosby Yard for three years when I decided to leave. I was anxious to get back to my writing, which I had put on the back burner since finishing my first book in 1975. What allowed me to do this was finding a job which was flexible and would allow me to write any day I chose.

My new job was for Hertz rental cars out of Hyannis Airport just 6 miles from my Centerville apartment. This job involved returning rental cars to the fleets of their original cities. We could work or not work anytime we wanted. Usually, four or five of us showed up on any given day. Most of the time we returned cars to Logan Airport in Boston, 70 miles away, coming back in the 10-passenger van we called the "turnaround car." At other times we'd do the reverse, retrieving cars and bringing them back to Hyannis. These fetching trips could go as far as the New York City airports 200 miles away. Sometimes we'd be on the road for 12 hours and drive 500 miles. The short Logan trips paid $25, the longer New York runs, $72.

Working for Hertz gave me the opportunity to set up a writing schedule. One day I would stay home and work on an article. On another, because I needed money, I would shuffle to Boston or New York. At the same time, my writing opportunities suddenly multiplied. Tom Jones, a good friend of mine, was an advertising salesman for *Cape Cod Life* magazine, a regional publication with a large readership.

Through Tom I was able to interest the magazine's publisher, Brian Shortsleeve, in assigning me an article about Nantucket. I called it "The Island Kingdom," and it was essentially a watered-down version of my book about the island's whaling history. The story received a good reader response, and Brian was so impressed that he commissioned me to write two more articles. This was the beginning of a long, fruitful association with *Cape Cod Life* that lasted 10 years, during which time I wrote 18 more articles.

While I was active with these jobs on the Cape between 1977 and 1982, my brother Donnie was going through his own transitions. He had started his own law firm of Williams & Brooke a few years back, and it was doing well. Things were different, however, at home. Lucia had given birth to two sons and a daughter. Since then their marriage had gradually gone downhill to the point where they decided to divorce. A year later, he was offered a job at the New England Merchants Bank as a legal counsel. In accepting the job, he had no idea he would meet someone who would change his life. And it happened in an interesting way.

Shortly after he had settled in Boston, an old childhood friend, Kenny Kunhardt, called him and told Donnie he knew a really "hot" available gal who happened to live in the area. Her name was Nancy. At 35, she was 14 years younger than Donnie, but Kenny gave him her number anyway and suggested he call her. Then, without my brother knowing, Ken called Nancy, telling her he knew a really "hot" 50-year-old who had just moved to Boston. Nancy wasn't particularly interested and refused to answer her phone for almost a week. But one time when it rang, she forgot and answered it. It was Donnie. The record has it that Nancy said, "Oh, no!" under her breath but relented and agreed to have dinner. Soon after this first date, they fell in love.

They were married in 1980, and I was my brother's best man. At the wedding I met Bunny, Nancy's sister. Bunny and I connected immediately and started seeing one another. Both of us were in the recovery program, which bonded us even more. Things were difficult at first because she lived in Biddeford Pool, Maine. So our relationship began over the phone. Occasionally, one of us found the time to make trips to Cape Cod or to Maine. But, eventually, common sense told me things would be much simpler if I just moved to Maine. I knew I could continue my writing there and I had confidence that I'd find a job.

Thus, I prepared for yet another move, leaving Cape Cod in 1982 and starting a new life in Maine.

CHAPTER 20

THE REUNION

I found an apartment in Cape Porpoise, a lobster town on the coast between Kennebunkport and Biddeford Pool, where Bunny lived. The town was a typical, small Maine Hamlet with a restaurant, a mom and pop grocery store with the post office in the back and a fleet of 20-odd well-kept lobster boats in its harbor.

Cape Porpoise was conveniently located for me – it was 20 miles south of Portland, 10 miles from Biddeford Pool and just 3 miles north of Kennebunkport. The grocery store was right across the street, the restaurant within walking distance and the waterfront and docks just a mile away.

After the first week of getting situated, I began looking for a job in the classifieds, and it wasn't long before I found one. A business called ServPro was offering a position. I had never heard of them, but the ad indicated it was a national cleaning company which paid a good salary. Calling the number, I was able to arrange an interview, and I drove up to Portland. When I came back that night, I had a job as a professional industrial and residential cleaner, work that I had no experience in nor knew anything about.

But I learned quickly. ServPro was one of the larger companies in the field, offering cleanup services for offices, partially burned buildings and residential homes. I worked with another employee named Ray, who was one of the managers. We drove a light green ServPro panel truck which was equipped with a large suction engine in the back, long length hoses and a variety of vacuums designed for upholstery, rugs and any other special surfaces.

On a typical day, two or three homes would be on the schedule. They were always located in residential areas outside Portland like South Windham, Scarborough and Falmouth Foreside. We'd arrive at a home, start the suction engine and pull the main vacuum hose through a backdoor into the house. After attaching the appropriate accessories, we were ready for cleaning.

There were two days in particular at ServPro that I'll never forget. The first was on a job in the upscale town of Falmouth Foreside. We were working in a beautiful trophy home which stood on top of a partially wooded hill overlooking the Atlantic. Ray was in the big living room cleaning the carpet while I was vacuuming the chairs and small sofa in the library. As I worked, I was admiring the many shelves filled with books when I noticed *Nantucket Then and Now* nestled in between some of them. I stopped working for a minute and thought of the irony. Here I was, a product of an upper middle class upbringing, the son of conservative Episcopalian parents and a Groton graduate, working as a carpet cleaner in a house similar to the one I was brought up in.

Just as I was thinking about this, the owner of the house walked into the library and nodded at me. He was wearing a Harris Tweed sport coat, grey flannels and loafers with no socks. Rummaging through a desk drawer for a minute, he started to return to the living room. I couldn't help myself and told him he had my book. He stopped, stared at me and then smiled almost sarcastically. So I reached up and pulled the book down from the shelf and showed it to him. Then I opened it and pointed to the inside leaf of the jacket where my author's photo was. His sarcastic expression changed into a curious one as he took the book from me and shuffled through its pages. Finally, he looked up and smiled, asking me how in the world a book author became a house cleaner. Then, handing me a pen, he requested I autograph it for him and apologized for not having read it yet.

The other memorable day was when I found out I had become a grandfather. Just before I moved to Maine, 20-year-old Lilli had met Allan Abrantes and they were married. She had become pregnant shortly after.

It was a June morning, and I was getting ready to go to work when my telephone rang. It was an overseas call from Lilli. She had just given birth to a baby girl who they named Penni. When I was on the job that day, I made it a point to tell everyone about my new rank in the world.

During my time off I was busy, too. Almost seven years sober now, I continued to be active in the recovery program. As on Cape Cod, I met a host of friends at meetings and had numerous opportunities to help newly sober alcoholics and drug addicts. One of the friends I met was Allen Pargellis who also lived in Cape Porpoise. It turned out he was a birdwatcher like myself, and we enjoyed a lot of time together out on the water and taking bird walks along Maine's rocky shore.

On the downside, my relationship with Bunny was in trouble. Not living together, we saw each other only every other day on average. Eventually, Bunny became interested in someone else, and our relationship came to a grinding halt. But our friendship had become strong, and I was grateful that we remained good friends and frequently saw one another at meetings.

For the next two years, I enjoyed my life in Maine. And I had every intention of remaining there indefinitely. But by then I ought to have known that relocation was becoming a pattern in my life.

It was the winter of 1984 when I was surprised to learn that my four children had decided to immigrate to the States. They planned to look for a place to live together in the New York City area. Actually, Ricky, now 20, had already come over and was living with an uncle in Texas. A short time after that, Lilli came to New Jersey with Penni where she was temporarily staying with a Filipino family. Philip, who was 18, and Caroline, now 17, were scheduled to fly into the Newark Airport together in April. So I began to plan another move. My hope was, being nearer to them, that they would want my support as they adapted to a new way of life.

My old *Yankee* shipmate and his wife, Jill, were living in Old Greenwich, Connecticut, which was not far from the city. We had kept in close touch over the years, and I felt comfortable asking if I could stay with them temporarily until I found a job and a place to live. They were delighted to have me and be able to help out.

Having arranged this, Allen Pargellis agreed to store my furniture in the old barn on his Cape Porpoise property. Consequently, it was a repeat scene of my past departures from Connecticut, Nantucket and Cape Cod. Breaking away from Bunny and the new friends I had made, I drove down to Jeb and Jill's in early March. It turned out I would remain with them for three months. I was fortunate to find a job nearby. It was with a limo company called Parlor Car which ran 25-passenger shuttle buses to the New York City airports. The runs started in Westport with stops at Darien, Stamford, and Greenwich and then straight onto La

Guardia and Kennedy. Parlor Car's terminal was in Norwalk just 15 miles up the Merritt Parkway from Jeb and Jill's.

It was an interesting job, paid well and offered substantial tip money. My passengers were mostly traveling businessmen who were always concerned they'd miss their flights. In the few times they did, they took it out on me, complaining because of my inability to fly over the congested traffic in front of us. The buses had television sets, free soft drinks and comfortable seats. But there was one amenity they didn't have—bathrooms.

This presented a problem, particularly for me. The route from Westport to the airports, making all the stops, usually was a one-and-a-half to two-hour drive. By the time I got to La Guardia, I began to feel the call of nature, which steadily grew as I dropped off passengers at the various terminals. But there was never enough time for me to jump out of the bus at these stops to relieve myself because the remaining passengers were always in a hurry to get to the next terminal. After delivering my La Guardia group, I still had no time. Now, I had to get back on the freeway and drive the 6 miles to John F. Kennedy Airport for my remaining people. When they had been taken to their terminals and I had an empty bus, there was yet one final obstacle. The airport police didn't allow me to take up any terminal curb space for even 5-minute stops.

Finally, after a month of suffering, I found an isolated spot at the end of a JFK runway. Using my bus as a partial blind, I jumped out and did what I had to do. I called this spot of relief the "Flying P Runway."

4

The prospect of seeing my children after 14 years was both exciting and terrifying. The guilt of leaving them when they were so young still haunted me. I was grateful that Jeb and Jill were around at the time to give their encouragement and support. It made the situation a little easier.

It was late March when Lilli arrived with Penni. For a time, she was to stay with relatives who lived in Mattawan, New Jersey, 50 miles south of Old Greenwich. I waited a few days to give her time to get situated, and then I called. We agreed that I would drive down the following morning and spend the day.

I lay awake that night trying to imagine what kind of a greeting I could expect. I wondered how much resentment and anger she might have towards me. What kind of a father was I to her? Had she forgiven me? Did she doubt that I loved her? I had a sleepless night. In the morning I got into my car and headed down the Merritt Parkway towards Mattawan.

My mind was racing wildly when I rang the doorbell. The last time I had seen Lilli she was a pretty 7-year-old schoolgirl, wearing a cute uniform, who I had taken to classes each morning. It was a 21-year-old Lilli who opened the door, holding my granddaughter in her arms. There was a smile on her face that was reassuring. We hugged for a long time, and then she led me into the living room.

As Penni made baby sounds and crawled on the carpet, Lilli and I talked and started the process of getting to know one another. I couldn't discern any anger or resentment towards me in her voice. She called me "Daddy" and reminisced about her life growing up in the Philippines and how much she had missed me. She shared that she had never given up hope and had always been confident she'd see me again. And she never asked me why I had left them so many years ago.

In turn, I talked about the guilt I still had for leaving them. I tried to explain to her why I had left, but the words didn't come out the way I wanted them to. I told her of the countless times I had thought about them, and the heartaches I had felt every time she sent photos of everyone as they were growing up. Our conversation went on for the whole morning and into the afternoon while Penni sometimes sat on my lap and stared curiously at me. Before I left, Lilli gave me some wonderful news. She had found a basement apartment in Queens that they would all move to the next month. How in the world she found a place, being a complete stranger and foreigner to New York City, I don't know and I didn't ask. But her resourcefulness amazed me.

Driving back to Greenwich later in the day, I realized how fortunate I was that Lilli had been so loving and responsive with me. Jeb and Jill were waiting when I arrived, and I remember excitedly telling them what had happened.

My meeting with Lilli was only the beginning. The following week Ricky, Philip and Caroline arrived, all at the same time, at Newark Airport. With Lilli at my side, we watched the passengers flood through the arrival gates. I was experiencing anxiety and joy at the same time, and I wondered whether I would recognize them from the photos I had seen of them growing up. Fourteen years is a long time, and they were just little children when I had left. But I shouldn't have worried because I picked them out right away.

What followed were hugs and tears. I got the same response from the boys as I had from Lilli the week before. But 17-year-old Caroline was quiet and withdrawn. I realized that she didn't even remember me. She was only two years old when I had left.

The following month they all moved into their Queens apartment. After that I saw them as much as I could. Once, I had the opportunity to bring Lilli and Ricky up to meet Jeb and Jill and spend the day. What I remember most about that visit was Ricky's first sight of a squirrel at a nearby park. There were no squirrels in Manila where he grew up. It was fun to see his exuberant reaction. On another occasion I took all four of them on a picnic in Manhattan's Central Park. It was a beautiful spring day with the dogwoods, cherry tree blossoms and daffodils everywhere. They seemed fascinated with these spring harbingers, and we took group pictures of each other with the flowers in the background. And I'll never forget the moment when I strode down Madison

Avenue with Lilli and Caroline on each arm, watching all the men turn their heads to look at us. I was so proud.

As the excitement of being reunited slowly wore off, a more normal life began. Lilli had a job as a secretary for a small business near Greenwich Village, but her salary wasn't enough to pay for the rent on their Queens apartment. So Ricky and Philip looked for work and, luckily, found jobs. Philip started work as a busboy at the Adam's Apple, a restaurant/bar on the East Side directly across from the famous Chippendale's nightclub. And Ricky found employment at a department store in the same area.

In the meantime, I finally moved out of Jeb and Jill's home and settled in an apartment in Trumbull, just north of Bridgeport, Connecticut. Besides relieving them of the burden of a prolonged visiting guest, my new place was conveniently close to the Parlor Car terminal in Norwalk, and it wasn't too far from Queens.

As I look back after so many years, I am more than proud of my children. What they accomplished in that first year in New York City was nothing short of a miracle.

Here you had a group of four young people. Completely on their own, they migrated from the Philippines, where they grew up, to a foreign country with an alien culture. They proceeded to find a place to live in Queens that they couldn't afford. Then they went out and got jobs in New York City, a place with a strange and sometimes hostile environment, and found jobs so they could survive.

To this day the courage they showed still amazes me.

PART III

CHAPTER 21

RETURN TO THE CAPE

I REMAINED IN Trumbull for the next year and a half, busy spending time with my kids and driving for Parlor Car. But a number of things were inextricably drawing me back to Cape Cod.

One of them was Dad's health. During his 80th birthday party in Nantucket, he had acted strangely. While all of us were in the living room, he went out onto the back terrace alone, sat down and stared into space for a long time. There had been other such incidents in the past, and this one just confirmed that Dad was experiencing the first symptoms of Alzheimer's disease. While I had been away, these symptoms had increased to the point where Mom had reluctantly put him in Our Island Home, Nantucket's only rest home. Because of this, I wanted to be closer.

I was also homesick for the Cape. When I was living in Maine, I had stuffed this feeling. But as time went on, the urge to return got stronger, and I couldn't ignore it. Thoughts of getting back to my writing and having more articles published in *Cape Cod Life* magazine became a big draw. The thought of writing again was compelling.

The third thing was the assurance, in my mind, that the children had made the necessary adjustments to their new lives in New York, and they were doing well on their own. And the Cape wouldn't be that far away, making it easy to visit one another.

Finally, I missed being near the sea.

Consequently, in the early fall of 1985, I made preparations for a return. But, as it turned out, there would be a short four-month stop on my way back. That's because I was offered a job as a limo driver for a big limousine outfit in Boston. I decided to take it temporarily because I needed the money. The job was made more attractive by the fact that Donnie and Nancy were now living in nearby Manchester-By-The-Sea. This would give me the chance to see them almost as much as I wanted. So I rented a motel room in Beverly which was just down the road from them and an easy commute to the limo office.

Despite a short period of depression, probably triggered by having a motel as an address, that fall and winter went well for me. I spent some quality time with my brother and sister-in-law. It was the first opportunity for me to really get to know Nancy, and I quickly realized what a pearl she was and a gold mine for Donnie. We had good times together, either eating at one of the many restaurants in the area or just hanging out at their home in Manchester-By-The-Sea.

The limo job wasn't so pleasant, and I had a couple of days I will never forget. One of them was when I was scheduled to pick up a lady and her daughter at the Hilton and take them around to see a few prep schools to help the young girl decide where she wanted to go.

To preface this particular trip, I will say that during my short career as a limo driver, I learned that all of my clients had one thing in common, *Money*. And they were generally represented by two groups. The first was made up of people who treated the driver as an equal. They would talk to you, ask questions and, seemingly, be genuinely interested in you as a person. Those in the other group carried a superior attitude that left no doubt that they thought their station in life was very much higher than yours. The limo driver was just part of the limo--almost an accessory. The mother and daughter clients on this job belonged to the latter group.

Dressed in my chauffeur's uniform, as usual, I pulled up to the front of the hotel at the agreed pickup time. I had not been waiting long when a neatly dressed mother and daughter appeared from the hotel entrance and got into my limo as I held the rear door open. Getting behind the wheel, I asked the mother where they would like to go first.

"Milton Academy," she said briskly, then slid the glass partition shut.

Milton was an easy 10-mile ride down I-93, and we were there in half an hour. As I dropped them off in front of the headmaster's house, the mother curtly informed me that they would be an hour or more. So I did what most limo drivers do best while waiting, I sat behind the wheel and daydreamed.

They returned later, and we went through the same formalities: I opened the rear door, went around and got behind the wheel and heard the glass partition slide open.

"Noble and Greenough, please." Then the partition slammed shut. I drove another 10 miles north to Dedham, arrived at the school and dropped them off. After 15 minutes they were back in the limo, and I waited for her next instructions.

"Now we're going to the Groton School."

The partition slid shut and my stomach turned. The last thing in the world I wanted was to drive around the circle of my alma mater in a limousine wearing a chauffeur's uniform. I, obviously, didn't want to be recognized, and as we were going there I thought of all the ways I could be inconspicuous.

Within the hour I found myself driving through the school's gates, around the circle and to the front entrance of the headmaster's house. Bill Polk was the headmaster then, and I knew him well. He had been in the class below me when I graduated in 1953. If he came out to greet my clients and saw me, who could say what his reaction would be. Groton's most famous graduate was President Franklin D. Roosevelt. This was a level of success that I, obviously, had not reached. Fortunately, he didn't come out, and the mother and daughter walked up the front steps and through the open front door. I stayed in the limo, praying none of the other teachers I knew would see me if they happened to walk by.

Two hours later we went through the gates again and headed back to Boston. This time the mother had left the partition open, and I heard her daughter talking about Bill Polk and the good opportunities he said the school had to offer. I couldn't hold back any longer.

"I am a Groton graduate, Ma'am."

There was a short silence. "Oh, really?" she finally said to my rearview mirror with a sarcastic smile.

"Yes. The class of '53." I went on to tell her about my connection with Bill Polk and what I thought were some interesting things about the school. She listened politely.

"Isn't that interesting," she commented after I'd finished and then slid the partition shut, making it very clear she hadn't believed a word.

An hour later, still trying to nurse my damaged ego, I dropped them off at the Hilton and went home. A few days later I figured it was about time for me to return to the Cape.

I rented a cozy, shaded cottage on River Road in Marstons Mills, a town 10 miles west of Hyannis and nestled in the hills of central Cape Cod. Even smaller than Cape Porpoise, the Mills was more a junction than a town, having just one mom and pop store and a nearby inn. This time, I was destined to remain on the Cape for the next 13 years. During these years I would enjoy the most productive period of my writing career by having 11 of my articles published in national magazines, such as *Cruising World* and *Yachting,* and an additional 18 articles appearing in *Cape Cod Life.*

A few months after I moved back, I got a job as a manager of a small company in Osterville called Sea Dune Limousine. It had just one stretch limo and one sedan. Most of its clients were local people from Osterville and surrounding areas. Sea Dune didn't advertise much, which made for a sluggish business. Most of the jobs were runs up to Logan Airport in Boston for drop-offs and pickups. Occasionally, we had longer trips to points around Massachusetts and Connecticut. What I liked most about the job was the free time it gave me. This was one of the reasons I was able to have so many articles published after I had settled in Marstons Mills.

And the free time also gave me opportunities to involve myself in other things.

Something that has always been very important to me is my spiritual growth and my relationship with God. I come by it honestly. As long as I can remember, Dad was always seriously committed to the Episcopal Church. His biggest contribution was his love for music, and he sang in the choir in every church we attended. Donnie had followed in his footsteps and, today, is not only involved with the church choir but also in the writing of arrangements for some anthems.

My interest in spirituality was no less, except I took a slightly different path. It started at Groton when I began to realize that I had problems with religion's rules. Instead, I wanted to practice my own beliefs rather than be told what those beliefs must be. The exception to this was when I had been baptized as a Catholic in the Philippines. At the time, I was an ardent churchgoer. However, looking back I now see that this activity provided a diversion from a bad marriage and an opportunity to preoccupy my mind.

Now, this path was leading me to the Unity Church in Hyannis. Unity was not so much tied down to doctrine as other organized religions, and it fit in nicely with my free-spirited beliefs. I became a regular member and, eventually, served on the board of directors. In addition, my spiritual growth was strengthened by the recovery program whose principles I had been now exposed to for more than 10 years.

But I had also been pushed towards metaphysical and paranormal areas through extensive reading and because of certain experiences I had in the past. During the last years of my drinking on Nantucket, I had become interested in the New Age movement and had read books (when I was sober enough) written by Ram Dass, Emanuel Swedenborg and others, which emphasized a spirituality and philosophy without borders and confining dogmas. And I studied Eastern religions and the practices of meditation and contemplation.

Later, during my sobriety, a number of incidents also had great influence in prodding me along this path. One of them was at the Nantucket hospital, during my detoxification, when I had had that sudden rush of pure hope. Another happened the day Ed Crosby died. As I arrived home from work that day, I felt his presence strongly and somehow knew he was invisibly standing right there beside me. And then, of course, there was the out-of-body experience I had at the podium in Brockton which changed something in me forever.

Perhaps, the most curious incident was that of the Red-Tailed Hawk. Donnie's longtime friend and matchmaker Ken Kunhardt passed away shortly after I had returned to Cape Cod. One morning a few days after Ken's funeral, Donnie walked into his 11th floor Boston office and saw a Red-Tailed Hawk perched on the window sill. This was highly unusual since this raptor's natural environment was the open country. Donnie passed it off as an unusual happening until he came into his office the next day and saw the same hawk on the sill again. This odd episode repeated itself every day for over a month. The significance of this is that

Ken was an avid birdwatcher, and his favorite bird was the Red-Tailed Hawk. It makes one wonder.

I think one of the greatest spiritual influences on me was my friendship with Katrina Gannon, a psychic I had met in 1978 at the Unity church in Hyannis. She was diminutive, pretty, 40-year-old woman who did past life regressions and, occasionally, predicted people's futures. She also organized trips to Egypt where she acted as a guide to all the sacred places. In addition, she had a meditation group which met once a week where she would do guided meditations and then afterwards had discussions about metaphysics and spiritual growth. For the 20 years I lived on the Cape, I would faithfully attend her weekly group sessions. From her I learned the value of meditation. Katrina became my spiritual advisor and mentor. And she still is; although, I see her rarely now.

I found my God as a result of all of these experiences and people and I became more in touch with my inner self and my humanness.

I had been back on the Cape for only a year when Dad died. He was 83. Fortunately, I had been able to go to Nantucket to visit him a few times. And, once, Lilli came up from New York with Baby Penni. When Dad saw the two of them, he said, "Lilli," and that was it. A moment later, as it is with Alzheimer's, Dad went off into another world and seemed unaware of our presence. As I recall, that was the last time I saw my father. He was buried in a cemetery which, ironically, was only 200 yards from my old walkup apartment with the 23 steps where I had spent my last years as an active alcoholic.

Life went on. Lilli and Allan (Penni's father, and a fellow Filipino) were married. Philip wedded a Puerto Rican gal named Gladys, joined the Navy and did a tour in the Persian Gulf on the aircraft carrier *Carl Vincent*. Ricky settled briefly in Vermont and attended college in Rutland. He also had a job at a ski resort, a huge transformation for a kid who was born and raised in Manila. And Caroline eventually moved to New Jersey with her new husband Sam, an American-born citizen of Egyptian parents. Except for Caroline, all the others would end up living in California by 1995.

As for me, I was busy with a number of things. One, of course, was my sobriety. Ever since my admittance to the hospital in Nantucket in 1976, I had not had a drink. As it is today, my involvement in the recovery program became a large part of my life. It offered me numerous opportunities to help others, and I was often asked to speak at large meetings throughout the area. I had made a host of friends, all who came from diverse backgrounds. I loved how this cross section of people shared a common bond.

I remained manager of Sea Dune Limousine. As the business grew, I took on another driver, my friend Tom Jones. And once in a while I shuttled cars for the Rent-a-car agencies out of the Hyannis Airport.

But despite all this going on, my thoughts increasingly centered around my desire to go back to sea again. Ever since I had sold *Marie Celine* 26 years before, this urge had never left me entirely. The mythologist Joseph Campbell often taught his students the wisdom of "following your bliss." Dad had done exactly that back in 1946 when, in his late 40's, he took the job of history teacher at St. Bernard's School. Now it was 1987 and I was 52 years old. Time was marching on.

What was stopping me from doing the same thing?

CHAPTER 22

DOWN TO THE SEA AGAIN

I was at the wheel of the brigantine *Romance* as she rushed through the water. The warm Caribbean trade winds on our quarter tousled my hair and filled the tier of sails aloft. Under all plain sail, we pushed through the darkness, and the bow wake up forward rumbled and hissed. Because we were miles from land, there wasn't any artificial light pollution, and the stars were sparkling dots on fire.

I was back. This was my first move to return to the sea again. Just before Thanksgiving of 1987, I wrote Arthur Kimberly a letter. I had read his ad in *Cruising World* announcing his two-week charters out of Tortola in the British Virgin Islands. His vessel was the *Romance*, a 110-foot brigantine which had been a legitimate sailing cargo carrier in the Baltic in the 1930's. It had been arranged that I would sail with him the second week in January. And although I was a paying client, I made it clear to him that, because of my experience, I wanted to be part of the crew, too.

So in January I had flown down to Road Town with high expectations. The *Romance* was anchored in the harbor, and I remember the excitement I felt as I jumped in the launch which brought me out to her. Arthur and his wife, Gloria, were at the gangway to meet me. They greeted me warmly, and I recall eagerly looking aloft at the high yards and feeling a flutter in my stomach. It was awesome to finally be back aboard a square-rigger again after almost three decades.

Now, we were into the second week of the charter, and I enthusiastically become part of the crew as I helped set and take in sail and stood watch with them. I had even thrown the lead line for depth soundings, the art I learned to love on board the *Yankee*.

But as a crew member, I had a surprise in store. It happened when I went aloft for the first time. Looking forward to being, once again, at my favorite place on earth - 50 feet above the deck surrounded by billowing sails - I confidently jumped into the rigging along with the rest of the crew. What I didn't expect was that when I reached the crosstrees, I was exhausted. I had forgotten that I was much older now and completely out of shape. Then I made the mistake of looking down at the deck below me. It seemed a mile away, and I felt an unfamiliar fear of heights I had not had when I was young. It took a few days to overcome this fear to the point where I could enjoy being out on the footropes helping the others take in sail.

I thoroughly enjoyed those two weeks. After 30 years, I had sat aloft and looked out over the sea again. I had gone out to the tip of the bowsprit and recorded the sounds of our tumbling wake. I had taken the wheel and sailed *Romance* as close to the wind as I could, keeping an eye on the shivering weather leech of the royal sail. And there were the voices of an old sailing ship that I loved so much - the groans and squeaks of the wooden hull as she rolled, the slapping of the rigging against the masts and the rattle of the anchor chain as the old bower anchor was let go. After three decades I was back in the world of the square-rigged sailing ship, and I didn't want to leave.

On the last night aboard, the crew gave me a gift. It was a piece of old canvas shaped like a square sail. On it written in paint read, "To Win Williams our honorary Bucko Mate." It was a gift which meant a lot to me and one I still have to this day.

After my 1988 cruise on *Romance,* there was no stopping me from getting back on the water. To start, I decided to go for my commercial captain's license. The United States Coast Guard required a minimum of 720 sea days for the Master 100-Ton license, the one I needed. Four hours underway constituted one sea day. With all my past experience, I had well over 1000. But 90 of the required 720 had to be what was called "recency sea time," that is, 360 days earned in the last three years prior to application. I had little of this time.

A year after I had sailed on *Romance,* an opportunity presented itself to take the first step towards accumulating these 360 days. Gary Blake, owner of Sea Dune Limousine, also had a 42-foot Bertram sport fishing boat. Besides managing the limo company, I was also expected to keep an eye on this boat which was tied up to one of the Crosby Boat Yard's slips. Gary usually spent the winter down in Palm Beach, Florida. This particular winter he wanted to have his boat available to use whenever he wished. So I was faced with the delightful job of bringing her down the inland Waterway, a 1000-mile trip. I called Jeb Kreimer in Greenwich and asked him if he would like to help me. He happily said, "Yes."

Gary emphasized there was no hurry, so we took almost two weeks. Having been given a fistful of credit cards, we had no worry about expenses like dockage and fuel. Jeb and I enjoyed this run down to Palm Beach. It was the first time we had been on a boat together since *Yankee* days, and it felt like old times being underway up on the flying bridge and cruising through the many backwater areas. At the end of each day, we'd have dinner at the marinas' restaurants and then talk into the night. On the last day of the trip, we were powering down the channel through

Jupiter, Florida, when we noticed an outboard boat catching up to us with two people on board who were waving enthusiastically. They turned out to be Jill, Jeb's wife, and a friend. This was a memorable end to an unforgettable two weeks with an old friend and shipmate.

During this period when I was busy accumulating sea time, I met Nancy Young, a woman a few years younger than me. We started going out together, and I remember our first date was at Wimpy's, Osterville's only restaurant. On our second date we went up to Boston to hear the Boston Pops featuring Sammy Davis, Jr. It wasn't long before we realized that there was something more than just friendship between us.

We were married on November 23, 1990, at the Marstons Mills Inn which, ironically, was a stone's throw from my snug little cottage. One of the most interesting things about the wedding was that it brought my kids and Donnie's together for the first time—a real icebreaker. It was a special experience to watch the seven cousins, from two different cultures, relate with each other. And I was happy to see Mom and Dad enjoying themselves. Mom seemed very approving of our marriage, unlike my first one to Lana.

It was a huge change for both of us. After her divorce from her first husband, Nancy had lived alone for a number of years, and I had also lived alone ever since 1969 when I left the Philippines 20 years earlier. But we were in love and that softened many of the more difficult adjustments we had to make during the first years of our relationship.

Settling down after the marriage, Nancy returned to her job as a legal assistant for a law firm in Osterville. I took the second big step towards acquiring the necessary sea time for my captain's license by accepting a job with Hy-Line Cruises out of Hyannis.

The line ran passenger vessels from Hyannis to Martha's Vineyard and Nantucket. Being one of the largest private companies of its kind on the East Coast, it had a fleet of five boats ranging from 100 feet to over 200 feet. It also had two harbor tour boats which ran out of the Hyannisport harbor and the Kennedy compound.

I became a deckhand aboard the *East Chop,* a 125-foot vessel with a capacity of 300 passengers. She made runs to Oak Bluffs on Martha's Vineyard 20 miles away and occasionally went to Nantucket. My job included taking hourly tricks at the wheel, standing bow watch in dense fog and cleaning up the boat at the end of the day. I usually worked with two captains, one commanding the two daily runs and the other, the only night run.

Sailing mostly on the day trips, I served under 74-year-old Captain Jim Hogan. He had spent his whole life at sea and was a mustached, serious looking man. Before Hy-Line, he had worked for the President Line and had been in command of several of the company's larger freighters and oil tankers. In World War II his first command as a young master had been a Liberty Ship. Jim did things the traditional way. You were expected to follow his orders without question and be reasonably quiet in the wheelhouse. If you were at the helm when he ordered a new course, you were expected to repeat it. He issued instructions calmly and confidently as you would expect any old salt to.

I liked him right away. Having read so much about maritime history and sailed in square-riggers before, I was familiar with and preferred the traditional ways and terms of the sea. From the first trip I took with him, he became my seafaring mentor. I loved working with him and couldn't wait to get to my job in the mornings, often arriving early. I was grateful to be back on the water again and to be paid for it at the same time.

During that first summer on the *East Chop*, I was given increasing responsibility. Jim was aware of my prior experience and saw my willingness to learn more. By August he was letting me use the radar as well as allowing me to plot our position on the chart.

The period between 1990 and 1993 was a productive one for me. Hy-Line only operated seasonally between May and October. This gave me the winters to concentrate on writing, and I sold 10 articles. Two of them were published by *Cape Cod Life* and the others by the national magazines *Cruising World* and *Sailing*. I even had one which appeared in the British magazine *Classic Boat*.

Sometimes Nancy and I visited Mom on Nantucket. Considering the fact that she was in her mid-eighties, she was still in good health. There were times when, as mothers are, she was loving towards me. But more often she criticized me for one thing or another, and I was relieved when we left and returned to the Cape.

In 1991 I received a call from Exy Johnson informing me that Irving had died. This had been expected since he had been suffering from Parkinson's disease the last few years. She asked me if I would be willing to give a eulogy for him at his funeral service in South Hadley, Massachusetts. To be asked to do this was one of the greatest honors of my life.

The second season I worked for Hy-Line, I continued to sail on the *East Chop* with Jim Hogan. My duties remained the same as the previous summer. However, there was one new routine. Jim began asking me at every Hyannis arrival to remain in the wheelhouse with him while he docked the boat. He explained he wanted me there to watch for traffic and to be ready should he need anything. Backing the 125-foot *East Chop* into the narrow slip between the two piers demanded skillful boat handling. As we made our approach, Jim would steer hard to starboard, making a U-turn until our stern lined up with the slip opening. Then, calmly leaving the wheel and walking out of the pilothouse, he would stand, facing astern, in front of a small throttle station next to the starboard rail. At that vantage point, he had an excellent view of our stern, the slip opening and the two piers on each side. Then, using the two small throttle and gear stick shifts, which controlled the engines, and shouting dock line orders to the crew, he would back the *East Chop* in until we were deep into the slip with our stern just feet from the waterfront bulkhead.

I had studied him and the other captains make this docking maneuver dozens of times. And it was good that I had because one day as we were approaching the Hyannis dock and Jim was about to make the U-turn, he turned and looked at me, nodded and then simply walked out of the pilothouse without a word. I stared at the vacant wheel for a few seconds before realizing he was expecting me to dock the boat. With my heart beginning to pound, I grabbed the wheel and spun it hard to starboard to start the U-turn. When the stern slowly rotated to the position where it was lined up with the slip opening, I left the wheel and walked out to the control area along the rail. Looking at the opening astern, I gently pushed the throttle back and *East Chop* began to creep backwards.

In front of me there were more than 50 passengers, all facing me as if I was on a stage. But unlike the experience I had had in Brockton 15 years ago, now my heart had stopped pounding, and I was more confident and focused. I gradually eased the boat into the narrow gap of the slip, then at the right time I shifted throttles slow ahead and at the same time ordered the stern spring line to be checked to stop *East Chop's* momentum. In minutes we were tied up with the passenger gangway in place. Feeling good and congratulating myself on my first landing, I watched people file off the boat down the gangway. Then I felt a tap on my shoulder and turned to see Jim Hogan.

"Well done," he smiled. I knew that was the highest compliment that he ever gave anyone.

One August morning that summer, before the *East Chop* departed on her morning run to Martha's Vineyard, I was called into Murray Scudder's office, the owner of Hy-Line. When I entered he got up and shook my hand, congratulating me. I had just been promoted to 1st mate.

The next day I exchanged my deckhand uniform of a red shirt and blue pants for a white shirt, a brass name plate with "Win Williams--1st Mate" on it and two black epaulets with three gold stripes. At 55 I was climbing up the maritime ladder.

The last two months of that summer in 1991 were one of the best periods of my time with the company. To my delight, I became Jim Hogan's 1st mate. It was no surprise that we worked well together. He now had me dock the boat regularly, in Hyannis as well as in Oak Bluffs. I was more involved with the radar and Loran navigation. Learning how to use radar was particularly important since Nantucket Sound was one of the foggiest areas on the East Coast. I got plenty of practice.

Occasionally, we had a celebrity on board. Once, Ted Kennedy and his wife were below on the main deck on an Oak Bluffs run. Out of courtesy, Captain Hogan asked me to go down and see if they'd like to come up to the wheelhouse. So I went below and introduced myself, inviting them to meet the captain. Kennedy smiled and politely declined, offering no reason.

Some of the night trips we took I remember fondly. They were special to me because I had the opportunity to watch the sunsets at sea. Then on the return trip, when the moon was full, I could see its shimmering path of light on the water. Often, these full moon nights made me think of sailing across the Indian Ocean on *Yankee* 33 years ago.

My third summer with Hy-Line was very much like the preceding ones. But there was one significant difference. After the Labor Day holiday, I had accumulated the Coast Guard's required number of 360 recency sea days. Now I could begin studying for my master's license examination in earnest.

Nancy and I made several trips to Nantucket to see Mom, who, at age 85, remained in good health. She was still living independently in the house on North Liberty Street and driving her car to get groceries. She also insisted on remaining in her old upstairs bedroom instead of moving to the first floor. We could not have guessed this insistence would lead to her death 12 years later.

Once we visited my old Groton roommate Bob Faesy in Maine who owned half of the island called Conary, located in Eggemoggin Reach in Penobscot Bay. Bob and his wife, Nancy, who had been a childhood friend of mine in Mendham, lived in a manner, and setting, everyone dreams about. Conary was between two small lobster towns called Brooklin and Sunset. The island was partially wooded and 100 acres in size. The house stood right on the water offering a beautiful view and the "station wagon" was an old lobster boat which was used to travel the 3 miles to town to buy groceries. They purposely didn't have a telephone. Their only communication with the outside world was a VHF radio. Its most common use was to contact incoming lobstermen to request a drop off of some lobsters on their dock for an evening meal.

On this get-away-from-it-all island, we picked wild strawberries that grew near the rocky shore below the house and gathered oysters in the shallow water around their dock. At night we would sit on their terrace and watch the stars, which stood out brightly because there wasn't any artificial light pollution, and we listened to the silence. To me their place and situation was the closest thing to Heaven there was on this earth.

Back home, Nancy and I attended Katrina's weekly meditation sessions and went to Unity church regularly. It was a blessing to discover that each of us were on the same spiritual path with the identical goals. And, as usual, I was seriously involved in the recovery program and now had 16 years of sobriety.

Life was being good to both of us.

CHAPTER 23

ON THE BRIDGE DECK

During the winter of 1993, after my third year with Hy-Line, I focused all my attention on obtaining my 100-Ton captain's license. Conveniently, a sea school designed specifically for those who were planning to take the exam, was located almost directly across the street from the Hy-Line offices. Called the New England Maritime School, it was run by a young couple named Jim and Lee Anne Hurley. Set up in what was formerly a motel, it had a number of classrooms and a front office which used to be the reception lounge.

The school had six computers, books, navigational tables, charts and whatever else was necessary for studying. It also held two classes a week teaching deck general subjects, navigation plotting and the rules of the road. The computers were available anytime during the day and were essential because they had dozens of certified Coast Guard tests you could practice taking to check your knowledge. Many of these tests were the actual ones used in the examination up in Boston.

I signed up with the Hurleys and started studying five or six hours a day. I attended the classes on deck general and also practiced my plotting navigation on the big charts in their chart room. When I returned to Hy-Line the following May to work for the new season, I couldn't spend as much time as I wanted at the school, so I brought books home and studied at night.

As far as my job went, there were some changes. Sadly, I was moved from the *East Chop* and Captain Hogan to the smaller harbor tour boats *Prudence* and *Patience*. The *Prudence* had been built in 1911 and was the oldest operating ferry in the United States. The *Patience* was much newer. Each was constructed of wood and had a passenger capacity of about 100. The tours were 45 minutes and scheduled every hour. Although I preferred to be on the *East Chop*, things were a little more laid back on the tour boats.

The big attraction on these harbor runs was the Kennedy compound in Hyannisport, which was right on the water. Ted Kennedy's schooner, the *Mya*, was moored just offshore from the house. Many times I would see him aboard, but I wouldn't point him out because I didn't want to disrupt his privacy.

While I was at the school on one of my days off, Jim Hurley casually remarked that after I had passed the exam and got my license, he might offer me a teaching job for one of his classes. I looked at him and remembered what I had always heard Mom say, "Don't count your chickens before they hatch." I had to pass the exam first.

And it was time. In September I made an appointment with the Coast Guard in Boston.

Dawn was just breaking as I merged onto Route 3 and drove north for Boston. Jim had advised me not to study for the last three days in order to clear my head. I had taken his advice. But, now, as I headed up the freeway, answers to hypothetical questions ran through my mind like a video in fast forward. I arrived at the regional exam center building an hour early at 7:00 a.m., parked in the adjacent lot and nervously waited in the car. Fifteen minutes before the test, I got out and walked towards the entrance to the reception area.

There were five or six applicants quietly waiting, and I sat down with them. At exactly 8:00, a uniformed Coast Guard officer opened a door and ushered all of us into a large room filled with desks. Each desk had a pile of reference books. I sat down at one of the desks and apprehensively waited to be given a test sheet.

The exam would take at least three hours, and it was divided into three parts. The first part was the rules of the road on which I had to score at least 90. The second part was deck general which included the subjects of weather, vessel regulations and boat handling. The third was navigation. The books on my desk were pilot and tide tables plus a volume called *Title 45 CFR*, which was a thick publication containing federal codes and laws pertaining to maritime subjects. Two-thirds of the exam was actually an open book test. The valuable thing I learned at Jim's school was the importance of knowing where to look up answers. Only the rules of the road part of the test was closed book.

The officer handed out the rules test first and then went back to his desk at the front of the room and sat down. There were 30 questions, and I knew I had to answer 27 correctly to pass. When I had finished, I walked up to the officer and handed in my sheet. He went over my answers while I stood nervously and watched. Then he glanced up, smiled and told me I had answered all 30 questions right. With that, he handed me the deck general test.

I returned to my desk with a little more confidence and began this next part of the exam. It was much longer and required a lot of time searching the books for answers. When done, I turned the test in and was then given a large chart of the Chesapeake Bay for the final navigation portion. I worked on the 10 problems by plotting positions and identifying buoys, using the available dividers and parallel rulers. When I finally finished, the clock on the wall read noon. I had been at it for nearly four hours. Going up front one more time, I handed in my plotted chart and was told to go out into the reception area and stay there until I was informed whether I had passed. For 30 excruciating minutes I sat with two others who had also finished. Finally, an officer appeared at the front counter and called my name, and I got up.

"Congratulations, captain!" he said, extending his hand and handing me my license. "Good luck and safe sailing."

I floated through the exit door and to my car. I remember cheering to myself out loud. The only other time I can remember feeling such joy and sense of accomplishment was when I had dropped *Marie Celine's* anchor in Taiohae Bay three decades earlier after 23 days at sea.

When I got home, the first person I called was Captain Jim Hogan.

Within days I was assigned to the *Patience*. My maiden trip as captain was surreal. I remember being nervous and at the same time enthusiastic. By the end of that 1993 season, I was confidently running the *Patience* and working with my crew. And to be frank, I secretly enjoyed the attention I got with my white shirt, captain's name plate and epaulets.

As he had said, Jim Hurley hired me as a teacher for the winter. I taught deck general and the rules of the road once a week on Thursday nights. I took to teaching just like Dad. There were about 10 students in my class, and they were a captive audience.

Each one was anxious to get his license, and they listened to every word I said. I'm proud that many of them did get their licenses and went on to run their own commercial vessels.

For the next five years I continued to work for Hy-Line. Most of the time, I was either running the *Patience* or the *Prudence*. During the trips, one crew member or I would do the harbor tour narration while the other would either stand bow watch or serve the passengers. Sometimes the run got monotonous, but I never stopped being grateful for my captaincy and being out on the water.

On Sundays we offered two very different runs. One was billed as the Ice Cream Cruise, and it was very popular. Hy-Line had made a deal with Haagen-Dazs who would deliver a huge container of ice cream packed in ice. Then we'd cast off and sail the routine harbor tour. This trip drew many families and their children. When we returned to the dock an hour later, the *Patience*'s decks were covered with puddles of Haagen-Dazs ice cream and empty containers.

The other run was billed as the "Jazz Cruise." Every Sunday evening from 6:00 to 9:00, we would meander around the harbor while a Dixieland jazz band played on the upper deck. The cruise was enormously popular with everyone, including myself. Often, I'd take the *Patience* out to Hyannisport to the rhythms of "Basin Street Blues" or "When the Saints Come Marchin' In." If the sea was smooth enough, I'd take us out beyond the breakwater into

Nantucket Sound. With the band playing and the sun setting, there were many moments I won't forget.

I had a second job, as well. This job was on a 65-foot schooner up on Provincetown, called the *Bay Lady*, which offered day sails out into Cape Cod Bay, and was owned by Bob Burns. I don't remember offhand how we met. But I do know that after going out with him a few times, he asked me if I would like to sail with him as part-time bo'sun. I said "yes" despite the fact that Provincetown was 60 miles from Centerville. Commuting up there twice a week was more than worthwhile.

Bob and I connected immediately. We both shared the same love of sailing traditional ships, and he knew the wind like an eagle. I recall many trips when the *Bay Lady* was running before a stiff southwest wind with Bob and I back at the wheel wearing enthusiastic smiles. I managed to sail with Bob a number of summers, despite my Hy-Line commitments. And I know that, had things turned out differently, I would have ended up working for him as an alternate captain.

In the mid-90's Jeb died of a heart attack. Nancy and I visited Jeb and Jill frequently after they had moved from Old Greenwich to Jupiter, Florida. He had shown no signs of heart trouble then or when the two of us had brought Gary Blake's boat down to West Palm Beach in late 1989. I have always had a curious memory of Jeb. During the world cruise, his daily job at sea was to peel potatoes. Each morning he sat forward peeling spud skins into an empty bucket between his feet. He often said his claim to fame was being *Yankee's* chief potato man. His death was a great loss for me.

During the same period, Nancy's mother, Gay, was diagnosed with lung cancer. She was a likeable and fun-loving person who was always a joy to be around. She was also very generous. Being told by her doctors that she had only a little time to live, she decided to have one last fling by treating her family of five to a two-week cruise from Panama to Barbados. We all had an enjoyable time, including Gay herself. A year and a half later she passed away.

On a lighter note, Mom celebrated her 90th birthday in 1996, and we organized a grand family reunion. Donnie had friends who were away on vacation at the time and who were willing to let us use their home in Hyannisport for the celebration. Everyone came: Donnie and Nancy; Donnie's children, Rowe, Merrill and Brad, who were now 42, 40 and 37, respectively; and Nancy and I with my children, Lilli, Ricky, Philip and Caroline at ages 33, 32, 30 and 29. Adding all the grandchildren, our number was close to 30.

Like our wedding earlier, it was a unique gathering of cousins from different cultures, although by now my flock had become somewhat Americanized. With Mom regally sitting at the head table during the big evening looking like Queen Elizabeth, my kids performed a number of authentic Filipino dances and songs. Donnie's crew put on skits spiced with choice tidbits about Mom's past, and he and I sang a duet together, with lyrics I had written about her life, with humorous anecdotes.

It was after this reunion when Lilli and Ricky moved to California. Philip was already there, stationed in San Diego with the Navy. Caroline was the only one who remained on the East Coast. She married a Wall Street broker, named Sam Bushrui, soon after the reunion, and they settled in New Jersey.

My job with Hy-Line continued for another three years while I was kept on the *Patience* and *Prudence*. By 1998 I had been with the company for nearly seven years, but my time with them was about to end.

Nancy's parents had lived outside Easton, Maryland, on their beautiful four-acre property alongside the Trappe River. It was a tranquil place, shaded by tall elm trees and adjacent to large corn fields with a quarter-mile long driveway. The house had a total of 5000 square feet of floor space, with added wings her parents had built when they first moved in. Nancy's father had already passed on and when Gay died, Nancy and her sister, Sally, inherited the property.

Because Sally and her husband, Fletcher, already owned a nice house in West Chester, Pennsylvania, it was principally Nancy's decision whether to move there or not. At the time neither sister wanted to sell the property. So after we had many discussions about what to do, Nancy and I decided to sell the Centerville house and move down to Maryland. It was too tempting. A lovely property sitting on the tributary of Chesapeake Bay laid waiting for us. And, as I found out later, there would be many opportunities for me to find work as a boat captain.

Twenty-four hours after we had put up the Centerville house for sale, it sold for the price we were asking. A week later I reluctantly gave notice to Hy-Line. The company had given me more than I could have hoped for in gaining experience and confidence as a captain. It was also sad to say goodbye to Jim Hogan and the Hurleys and their school, to all my recovery program friends and to Katrina Gannon, who had become an important part of my spiritual life as well as Nancy's.

The day finally came when we packed up and moved to Maryland. It was early 1998, and I was 62 years old. A new chapter in my life was about to begin.

CHAPTER 24

CHESAPEAKE COUNTRY

NEVER HAD I had a job where I could commute to work on my 19-foot outboard boat. From our dock, down to the Trappe River's mouth and on up the Tred Avon to Oxford was a mere 5 miles. I had landed a job as a captain for the Oxford-Bellevue ferry, reportedly the oldest operating ferry route in the United States. Their sole vessel was a 9-car ferry which crossed the mile span of the Tred Avon between the two towns.

This was only a part of my remarkable life with Nancy in Maryland. Our four-acre property and three-bedroom home was scenic and quiet. Shaded by the old elm trees, the large back lawn stretched down to the Trappe River's bank. Located at the water's edge was a dock where I could tie up my boat. In front of the house was a circular driveway with a hedgerow and cornfield on one side and a large lawn on the other. A swimming pool on the west side of the house offered a nice outdoor lounging area.

It didn't take us long to adjust to this beautiful setting. After living in a much smaller house on the Cape, it was nice to be able to roam around the 5000-square-foot floor space of our new home. Living in such conditions, it was easy to adapt to our new Maryland life. Besides my job in Oxford, I went to the many recovery meetings in the neighborhood and met a host of new friends. Nancy found a secretarial job in nearby Cambridge and also became involved in volunteer work.

I ran the Oxford-Bellevue ferry three times a week. This vessel was a real challenge in boat handling for me because she had propellers on each end. This meant that your bow going over to the Bellevue side became your stern returning to Oxford. Handling the vessel was done by two sets of controls located opposite each other in the wheelhouse. After you arrived at one dock and waited for all the cars to be driven aboard, on the return trip you simply did an about face and used those controls in front of you. When entering each slip, you used the bow engines to brake the vessel to a stop. All this required disciplined coordination.

And because the crossing was so short, it seemed that you were docking constantly.

With help from David Bittner, the owner, I was broken in to the point where I became accustomed to the ferry's idiosyncrasies and was able to handle her with some confidence. I had someone else working with me who directed traffic at each dock, waving cars off the boat and directing new ones on to specific spots in order to carry as many as possible.

The commute from the house was 4 miles by road. If I wanted variety, I'd take my outboard instead. I was scheduled for Tuesdays, Thursdays and Fridays, my first trip being at 7:00 a.m. and the last at 1:00 p.m., at which time I was relieved by David himself. My lunch usually consisted of one sandwich, a bunch of grapes and a Diet Coke. I rarely got a break and, most of the time, had to eat on the run. Sometimes people would ask me how long it took to get from one side to the other. I'd always answer "one sandwich," which meant there was barely time to eat one before I was busy landing the ferry on the opposite side.

I also became a captain for Chesapeake Marine Tours in Annapolis. Like Hy-Line, this outfit was one of the largest privately owned commercial boat businesses on the East Coast. The company owned four large vessels (up to 150-feet long), three smaller ones and a number of water taxis. These boats ran harbor and river tours, day runs (27 miles down the Chesapeake to St. Michaels) and night charters. The company offices were located at the city's main wharf adjacent to the U.S. Naval Academy. When

I went to work for them, I didn't realize it would turn out to be the best job I would ever have as a captain.

I had to like working for them to be willing to drive 130 miles round trip from home. And I had to juggle my schedule with the Oxford-Bellevue job. What I loved most about Chesapeake Marine was that I would be assigned to run any one of four boats. My employment was never dull and, happily, I was able to fit in two or three days a week with them.

There were two boats of the fleet that I ran most of the time. The first was the 85-foot *Harbor Queen*. The *Queen* did 45-minute tours around Annapolis Harbor and, occasionally, up the Severn River. She was a model of the old Mississippi paddle wheelers with a big wheelhouse and fake twin smoke stacks.

The second boat was the 65-foot, 90-passenger *Annapolitan*, which offered one-day cruises down the Chesapeake to St. Michaels on the Eastern Shore, a trip which took three hours. Both boats had a lunch bar where snacks and drinks were available. Rarely, I would also run the 55-foot *Providence*, another river boat type which was used exclusively for charters.

The *Annapolitan* was by far my favorite. More than any other boat in my maritime career, she brought out the strongest sense of captaincy in me. There were a couple of reasons for this. First, I was actually taking passengers to a specific destination rather than making the same trip six times a day around a harbor. Second, the 27-mile run to St. Michaels was a challenging one, testing my navigational skills with different changes of course. The final reason was that sometimes we had thick fog which forced me to rely on my radar and Loran experience gained at Hy-Line.

Also, the *Annapolitan* run required a lot of boat handling on each end. The approach to the St. Michaels pier was confined and tricky. At Annapolis, I had to back into a narrow slip with a crosswind similar to the situation with the *East Chop* in Hyannis except it was twice as difficult. I loved the docking challenges and must admit that most of my landings were good ones. Sometimes they were even rated. While bringing the *Harbor Queen* alongside the Annapolis pier, for instance, several employees, standing by the office building, would hold up cards with numbers on them judging my landing just like the judges of the old figure skating competitions. Once, I got a 4, more often an 8 or 9 and, occasionally, a 10. This game made docking the *Queen* a small adventure.

It was the year 2000, and Nancy and I had been in Maryland for just a year. Life was going well and, at age 65, my general health was good. To insure it, I had started to take regular morning walks down our half-mile driveway and back. After doing this for a while, I slowly developed mild pain in my left elbow when I walked briskly. I passed it off as the bursitis I had had for a number of years. However, one Saturday afternoon, I felt it while just sitting in the living room.

That same night, I went to my usual Saturday recovery meeting in nearby Easton. After the meeting a few of us decided to go to Denny's for some ice cream where I ordered a rich butterscotch and fudge sundae. I had half-finished it when one of my friends next to me remarked, "Don't you know that stuff will kill you, Win?" We both laughed.

On my way home, I began to feel chest pains. When I got to the house, the pains had grown worse, and I broke out in a cold sweat and was short of breath. Nancy didn't hesitate and called 911 right away. An ambulance arrived 15 minutes later, and I was taken to Easton Hospital where the doctors examined me and determined that I had had a mild heart attack. A blocked artery was the cause. The next day I was taken up to a Baltimore hospital where an angioplasty was performed and two stents were placed where the blockage occurred. In four days I was home again, and I recovered rapidly. Within three weeks I was back at work.

From what the doctors said, there were two things that possibly saved my life. The first was after I got home that night, I immediately took some aspirin. The second was Nancy urging me to take deep breaths while I was sitting and waiting for the ambulance.

Mom, now 93, decided she wanted to visit us in Maryland while she was still healthy. Taking the boat to Hyannis from Nantucket, she was picked up by Donnie and Nancy, who had also wanted to come, and all three drove down. Since they were coming, I asked my children, too. Lilli, however, was busy in San Francisco, and Caroline was tied up in New Jersey. But Phil, who was on leave in Norfolk, and Ricky, who flew from California, joined the rest of us. We had a good week together. Mom seemed to be enjoying herself, too, although she was upset by a few minor things, as usual.

We had dinners in our formal, unused dining room and appreciated the meals Nancy laboriously cooked. I took everyone out on the boat, touring Oxford and Cambridge. And to make Mom's visit more interesting, we drove her around the area and took her out to some of the finer restaurants in the area. After the week was up and everyone was gone, Nancy and I readjusted to what seemed like a quieter house than normal.

I don't know when it was that I became aware of an uncomfortableness. Nancy and I had experienced the usual rough spots that couples normally have in marriages. But some of our differences started to corrode the relationship.

One area was about possessions and money. As far as possessions were concerned, I felt that now, being married, what we had each owned before became mutual property. She believed that her past possessions, like the car she'd always owned, was still exclusively hers. This led to considerable stress.

To her credit, Nancy definitely managed money better than I did. She always had her checkbooks balanced and knew what we could or couldn't afford. She was appropriately cautious. By contrast, I rarely planned finances, had no savings account and rarely balanced a checkbook. This caused a growing friction between us. As I look back, had I been more like her, I may have saved myself from getting into the serious financial problems I was to face later.

Much more basic, however, was a part of my character which was deficient of testosterone. There, I lacked the aggressive and take-charge type of personality. This was ironic because, as a boat captain, I was responsible for as many as four crew members. It was part of my job to take control, tell them what to do and teach them the basics of seamanship. But when I came home and laid down my captain's hat, I transformed into an accepting, pliable person who was more willing to please than to be assertive.

This part of my nature had a good side. My friends considered me a friendly, patient and agreeable person. But then there was the other side. And that was my tendency to give up control—to allow the other person to take the reins. In our relationship, this translated into forcing Nancy to cope with nearly all of our responsibilities, ones I was more than happy to turn over to her. As a result, she ended up handling our money and making most of the decisions while I sat back unconcerned. This didn't help our relationship any.

Perhaps the biggest cause of our declining marriage was my inherent desire to be independent. This sense of free-spiritedness had had an enormous influence on me since childhood, starting with my *Yankee* dream, continuing with the *Marie Celine*, living in the Philippines, breaking away from alcohol and finally setting out on a seafaring career so late in life. And, like it or not, it also was the reason I secretly wanted to live alone.

There was much more involved in our relationship than just this. But it finally all came down to my wanting to separate. And there was a place where I could temporarily stay. Since 1992, Nancy and I had gone to Florida every winter to visit Jeb and Jill. Later, we rented an apartment of our own. Finally, we purchased a condo in Jupiter. This condo was the answer.

I know Nancy suspected something was up. She didn't seem too surprised when I announced I wanted a trial separation and that I'd like to stay in the Florida condo for a few months. Of course, at first she resisted. But soon she realized I was determined to go through with it. Any doubt in her mind about this was destroyed when I came home one late afternoon and told her I had resigned from both my Annapolis and Oxford jobs.

Sometimes we make decisions in life which we will never understand. In this case, I wonder why I chose Florida. Why couldn't I have just rented an apartment in Annapolis and continued captaining the *Harbor Queen* and *Annapolitan*, a job to this day I loved more than all the others?

During my last days in Maryland before my departure, a strained silence took over the house. We moved about and didn't talk much. There were no heated arguments, no fights. Sometimes you could cut the atmosphere with a knife.

The morning I left was surreal. Nancy cried when we said goodbye. I got in the car with all my suitcases in back and slowly drove down the long driveway. I watched Nancy's profile in the rearview mirror get smaller and smaller. It was July of 2000, and after 10 years of marriage I was finally headed for Florida—alone.

Deep in my mind I knew I wouldn't return.

CHAPTER 25

FLORIDA

There are few places which have bluer water than the Atlantic Ocean off Juno Beach, Florida. I was sitting in the Ciera late one afternoon shortly after I had arrived in Jupiter. Looking out over the sea's intense color, I was reviewing the events of the last month.

I realized my marriage to Nancy was over the moment I had started the car and was going down that long driveway in Maryland. And although she might have played her part in this, my free-spiritedness, more than anything else, was also to blame. The dream machine I'd always had was still alive and well. Now it had created a conflict of guilt and relief at the same time.

I knew I had to make some decisions soon. I had already made a few. One was that I would file for divorce in September, a month away. I wanted a little time, to be certain, before I went through with it. Another was that I would stay in our Jupiter condo only temporarily until I found a place of my own to rent and a captain's job.

Having made these decisions, I concentrated on the business of settling in. One thing that helped me in this process was the fact that Jill lived only a short distance away. Her presence was a great support. And through her, I made friends who helped me adjust to my new surroundings. Also, attending recovery meetings around the area gave me the chance to meet even more people with whom I felt a strong commonality and connection.

But it still wasn't easy in the beginning. September came and, with it, the difficult and stressful call to Nancy to tell her I wanted a divorce. During this conversation she was understandably emotional and resistant. The call had its effect on me, as well. The next day I fell into a depression accompanied with panic attacks so bad that I had to go to a doctor. Thankfully, I had recovered enough in two weeks to be able to make additional calls to her, and gradually she began to accept the inevitable. I tried to make things a little easier for her by offering to give her my half ownership of the condo. But overall, it was just a rough period with stress and tension.

Meanwhile, I began looking for a job. It turned out to be a frustrating search. I found one company which owned a 60-foot tour boat which ran trips up and down the inland waterway north of West Palm Beach. The owners went so far as to check out my boat handling skills. It was, however, one of those situations when they expected one of their captains to resign soon, opening up a position for me. But they didn't know when, so nothing came of it.

Another potential job was running a pontoon tour boat up the Loxahatchee River, which winds through the Jonathan Dickinson State Park northwest of Jupiter. But that turned into a "we-will-hire-you-in-the-near-future-when-we-get-a-little-more-organized" type situation. So then I decided to drive down the 20 miles to West Palm Beach and look for a possible job on one of the boats working Lake Worth. Nothing happened there either.

During the years when I lived on the Cape and in Maryland, my brother had enjoyed a successful career as a lawyer and ended up being Trust Council for his bank. After retiring, he and Nancy moved to Naples, Florida, where they purchased a condo in Pelican Bay just north of the city. There were three good friends, I had known for years on Cape Cod, who had also moved to Naples. So I took a break from my job hunting and drove the 90 miles across the state and stayed with my brother and sister-in-law for a week. It turned out to be an eye-opening visit.

We had fun together, eating out, going to the beach and just hanging out in their condo. Also, I discovered that there was a recovery club nearby which held meetings daily. And I was able to get together with my Cape Cod friends, Jim Fisher, Oona Conroy and her husband, Vincent, and Dick Tully.

During the Sunday I was there, I went to the Unity Church service with Donnie and Nancy. It was held in one of the most beautiful and original church buildings I had ever seen. Located in the woods near a quiet pond, it was a large, circular structure which had windows stretching the entire circumference, and it was covered with a gold dome. Inside, no matter where you sat, these windows allowed you to see peaceful trees and the pond beyond, and light burst in, making its interior bright and cheerful.

The service was interesting, too. I was moved by the sermon given by Jack Kern, the minister. He had a wonderful sense of humor, which came out in the stories he told to illustrate his points. Donnie was a member of the choir as he had been for every church he had ever attended. He made me think of Dad, who had done the same thing.

Going to that service rekindled my urge to work on my spiritual growth, something I had often neglected since Cape Cod days and Katrina's meditation group. When I found out Jack Kern held his own sessions on Tuesday nights, I decided to go. I was glad I did. I would never have thought I'd like a group better than Katrina's. I was dead wrong. Jack proved to be an excellent teacher and did an inspirational guided meditation. I promised myself to come back and go to another one of his meditation sessions the next time I was in Naples.

And then there was the recovery club. It thrived with activity, and I loved it. One day I was asked to speak, and I shared my 25 years of sobriety that began with that life-changing day at Nantucket hospital when Mickey and Sue had visited me and had given me so much hope.

My week in Naples ended and, as I drove back to the East Coast, I thought about the possibility of moving to Naples. It offered so much, whereas, Jupiter had been a struggle. I would have to get out of the condo eventually, and I still hadn't found a job. Having my brother and old friends from Cape Cod living in Naples was a strong pull. There was the Unity Church that I was so impressed with and Jack Kern's Tuesday night group, too. And Naples seemed to offer more work opportunities than Jupiter.

Probably what pushed me into making a final decision to leave Jupiter was when the Ciera's engine blew a week after I got back. It cost me $3000 to have a rebuilt engine installed, which proved to be a drastic hit on my bank account. That was the last straw. I would move to the West Coast

So, I made two trips back to Naples, finding a nice apartment on Vanderbilt Beach Road, just 3 miles from Donnie and Nancy's condo. I sealed the deal by putting down a deposit.

Those last days in Jupiter were difficult for me. It wasn't because I was anxious to get to Naples but because of the fact that, by leaving our condo, I was taking the last physical action to separate myself from Nancy. Our condo brought back memories of the last 10 years. I would spend the evenings out on the small terrace looking back on the good memories. I remembered the many peaceful spring evenings in Maryland when the wood thrushes would sing their flute-like songs. Nancy and I would even take a ride in the car sometimes and stop alongside the borders of forests, turn the engine off and listen to them in silence. I thought of the times we both went out on my boat up the Trappe River or down 7 miles to Cambridge to have dinner. Those last evenings in Jupiter were ones of many mixed emotions. The finality of our pending divorce was beginning to sink in. But all these things now were in the past. I had to turn my attention to what was in front of me.

Leaving Jupiter in October, I drove across the state to Naples and my new apartment. As I was driving, I did some counting and realized this would be the 9th major move I had made since I went to Hawaii the fall after the *Yankee* world cruise 42 years earlier. Now, it was the year 2000. Most people spent their entire life in one or two places.

If this were a relocation competition, I would be right up there near the top.

CHAPTER 26

NAPLES

A FTER HAVING such trouble getting a captain's job in Jupiter, it was a surprise when I was able to find one right away in Naples. It was with the Lady Brett Company, which owned one boat called the *Double Sunshine*, a twin-hulled, 50-foot harbor tour vessel. She ran 45-minute tours around Naples Bay and dolphin watching trips out at the harbor's entrance in the Gulf of Mexico. She also went on sunset cruises. The company's dock and ticket office was located in Tin City, an area in town with a cluster of gift shops and restaurants bordering the waterfront.

The company was owned by a strict no-nonsense gentleman named Gene who insisted everything was done his way right down to the proper method of taking cash from a customer's hand. I had met him briefly and left my resume. Two days later he called to tell me I was hired.

The *Double Sunshine* was tied up just 6 miles from my new apartment, making it an easy commute and a far cry from the 65 miles I had to drive to Annapolis the year before. The day's first trip was at 10:00 and the last was the sunset cruise. Each harbor tour was narrated. I was familiar with narrations, both recorded and live. During the recorded ones, as on the *Harbor Queen*, it was always a question of timing so that you were at the exact spot the recording was talking about. Live narrations, as on Hy-Line's *Patience* and now *The Sunshine*, were easier but had to be memorized.

The first week of the job I went along on the trips to listen to the other captains and took notes of their narrations. Before long I had memorized the spiel and was doing it using my own style. The trips varied one from another because Naples Bay had so many inlets and coves to explore. But one part of the tour was always the same and that was going out Naples' Pass into the Gulf of Mexico where we saw the dolphins.

Depending on the day, my one crew member and I could have as many as 50 passengers, most of them preferring the upper open deck. I would take the *Sunshine* up the inlets to see the many elegant homes owned by the wealthy and certain celebrities. Going out into the Gulf, we would watch the dolphins and look down the Florida shoreline, which stretched north all the way to Fort Myers and south to Marco Island. When we returned to the dock, there was already a line of passengers waiting for the next trip.

The sunset cruises were my favorites. Without having to do the narration, I could relax and enjoy taking the *Double Sunshine* out through the pass and into the Gulf. There, I would just drift quietly as the sun went down. Sometimes, the sunset was so spectacular that the passengers would applaud as the sun disappeared below the horizon.

Some of the passengers were particularly interested in seeing the "green flash." This phenomenon happens when certain atmospheric conditions combine to cause a green flash to erupt as the sun goes down. Despite all the time I spent at sea in my life, I had only seen one. And during my time with Lady Brett and *Double Sunshine*, we didn't see any.

I enjoyed the job. Unfortunately, though, I had a real problem getting along with the owner Gene. It got to the point where I dreaded coming to work. Because of this, I began looking for another job.

A rumor was going around the waterfront that one of the most affluent and beautiful golf course communities in Naples was looking for a boat captain. Called Windstar on Naples Bay, it was a large gated community on the east side of the bay and just south of downtown Naples. Featuring a Tom Fazio designed course, tennis courts, a marina and yacht club and elegant homes, it was a sought-after place to live by the well-to-do.

One of its most interesting features was a stretch of beach on the barrier island of Keewaydin, 4 miles south towards Marco Island. A 25-passenger pontoon shuttle called the *Keewaydin Queen* ran scheduled trips from the Windstar dock, down the inside channel through an undisturbed mangrove estuary to the club's private resort on the island. From a small dock, a 100-yard path meandered across the island and ended at the beach on the Gulf side. Facilities included a large screened pavilion, with a generator to power the lights and the fans, beach chairs and two outhouses.

Windstar's current captain was retiring, and they were looking for a replacement. Offering much more money than Lady Brett, I applied, was interviewed and offered the job. So I gave Gene notice, knowing I might miss running the *Double Sunshine* but not miss being told the exact manner I should take money from a customer's hand.

I had no idea what to expect working on an outboard pontoon boat. It seemed like I was taking a step down after being captain of 300-passenger vessels in Maryland. On the other hand, I was getting a better income and wouldn't have to work for a boss I didn't get along with.

My time with Windstar was a very different experience from any captain's job I had had before. Round trips to Keewaydin and back were scheduled for 10:00 a.m., noon and 2:00 p.m.,

Wednesday through Sunday. And being the boat's captain wasn't my only duty. I had the responsibility to maintain the club's private Keewaydin beach area. This included taking care of the generator, seeing to it that the pavilion and bathrooms were clean and making sure all the beach chairs were accounted for. In addition, I had an office at the clubhouse where I took reservations called in by Windstar members for future trips and kept records of previous ones. I had to be careful that I didn't overbook any one trip which would exceed the 25 passenger limit of the *Keewaydin Queen*.

The most popular run was the noon trip. On an average I would have 10 to 12 people; although, sometimes I'd get a full load of 25. Some came just to enjoy the boat ride and would go back to the club on the return trip. Others would stay all day until the final 4:00 p.m. return. It was important that I made sure there weren't any more than 25 left on the island for the final return trip of the day. My biggest worry was that I would leave one or two people behind.

The 4-mile runs out to the island took 35 minutes, and the highlight of every trip was the wildlife. One popular attraction was the Ospreys. They were common residents of Florida and built their nests on top of the channel day markers. In late winter they'd lay their eggs and, while they roosted, you could see the head of one of the parents sticking up above the nest's rim. This was an everyday sight until mid-April when there was an interesting change. Now, in addition to the parent's head, there would be two or three smaller heads of the chicks. As the weeks went by, these young Osprey grew quickly until they were larger than their parents. At this point these now fully grown juveniles would be precariously balanced on the edge of the nest, flapping their big wings. Inevitably, they would risk taking their first short flight. It was almost comical to watch them as they awkwardly attempted to make their first landings on the tree branches lining the channel.

The Ospreys were only part of the wildlife show. We would also see Great Blue Herons, Snowy Egrets and Tri-colored Herons in abundance. Sometimes, even a majestic Bald Eagle would glide overhead, displaying its dramatic black and white patterns. And for striking colors, there was no bird in Florida more spectacular than the Roseate Spoonbill whose radiant pink feathers glistened in the sunlight. By contrast, we always saw mean looking alligators that remained half-submerged and motionless, lurking in the mangrove swamps.

But the most popular sight by far was the dolphins that sometimes approached the *Keewaydin Queen*. I learned a trick to induce them to perform for us. A characteristic of the dolphin is its love of following in the wakes created by boats. I found that the slower I ran the *Queen*, the larger my wake became. This seemed to entice these large fish to playfully surf on the wave's curl and, occasionally, jump completely out of the water and fall back with a dramatic splash. This show might last as long as 5 minutes to the delight of my passengers.

What with managing and maintaining the Windstar beach resort, booking reservations at the office and keeping to the schedule of round trips to the island, my job kept me very busy. Fortunately, the two days off I had gave me some time to myself.

One of the reasons I moved to Naples was to be near my brother and Nancy. It was a short 10-minute drive from my apartment to their condo in Pelican Bay, and I took advantage of it. Often, we'd spend an afternoon on the beach together or we'd go out for dinner. Other times, I just hung out with them at their condo.

Donnie and I had always enjoyed a close friendship. This was interesting because we had led opposite kinds of lives. He had been the conventional brother, completing college, becoming a lawyer and having a successful career in the corporate world. I, on the other hand, had been the "black sheep," pulling out of college, sailing around the world, savoring a few youthful years in Tahiti, spending inheritance money on a schooner and living in the Philippines. But it was this very difference, I think, which pulled us together. I believe there was a part in each of us which envied the life of the other.

I loved Donnie's talent as a musician. He had played wonderful jazz since he was very young, and his talent only grew as he got older. He could also sing and write musical arrangements. As I mentioned earlier, there was never a church he had gone to where he wasn't in its choir. Currently, he had become part of a quartet in Naples which sang in hospitals and retirement homes to entertain the patients and retirees. Lastly, he was a tenor in a prestigious group of 80 vocalists, called the Voices of Naples, who put on concerts around the state.

The fact was we simply meshed. I can't ever recall having a serious fight with him. There were disagreements, like the time I was about to purchase Kellum's plantation in Moorea. And sometimes he had been a little mean to me when we were kids. I remember when I was six years old, he used to terrify me by hooting through the heat ventilators in our Mendham house while I was taking my compulsory afternoon nap. But I have forgiven him for that. Little things like this were only normal bumps in the road in a strong brother-friendship bond which has lasted a lifetime.

The old friends I had known on Cape Cod who now lived in Naples were another reason I had moved to Naples. Jim Fisher, Oona and Vincent and Dick Tully had all migrated from up north. I had known Oona for years, even before she married Vincent. She was a wonderful Irish gal who had lived in the States for decades and never lost her charming accent. Actually, we had a date long before Vincent had even met her. I asked her for dinner at my modest Marstons Mills cottage one night. Hoping to impress her by doing some first-class cooking, I had laboriously cooked a Stouffer's frozen dinner. Of course, she was far from impressed. We've joked about that night ever since.

And because of the recovery meetings, which had helped me stay sober now for 26 years, I had met a host of new people. One of them was very special. He was Father Joe. Next to Paul Carrier, Joe became one of my closest friends.

He was the head of the largest Catholic parish in Naples. All of his parishioners called him "Father," as was expected of them. But when he got in the recovery program, he was simply called "Joe" by everybody. He loved this because it put him on the same level as everyone else. For a change, he wasn't put on a pedestal. Another thing he liked about the program was its spiritual aspect. I'll never forget the meeting when he confessed something in front of the group. At 65, he'd been a priest for 40 years, he said. How many confessions, sermons and masses had he experienced in that time? Yet, despite all of this, he admitted he had never really known his God until he got into the program. I have been inspired by this admission of his ever since.

The Unity Church inspired me to work on my spiritual growth, too. I have never been a consistent churchgoer because I have always been uncomfortable with doctrines and dogma. As someone described it, I was not "churchy." But I became active in Unity because it was more liberal and didn't have many "does" and "don'ts." God wasn't a Being in the sky who was capable of anger, but within and around each of us. And Unity believed that the True Church was the state of consciousness in mankind.

I was very active at Unity and never missed Jack Kern's guided meditations. My involvement in it made my few years in Naples a very meaningful period.

One morning when I was driving to work, I began to feel chest pains. Making a U-turn, I went straight to my doctor. And it was a good thing I did. An angiogram showed a significant blockage in one artery. Donnie immediately drove me up to the hospital in Ft. Meyers, and the next day I had an angioplasty where a stent was placed in that artery. I stayed in the hospital for two days and then was discharged and sent home. It took two weeks to recuperate and be strong enough to go back to work. Fortunately for Windstar, a club member who had extensive experience in handling boats was able to cover for me while I was away.

All the time I was in Naples, my children were in touch with me regularly. All of them had settled in California except for Caroline and Sam, who lived in Mattawan, New Jersey. Ricky and Jill Ann, his wife, were in Sacramento where Ricky was working for a bank as well as involved in starting a real estate company with Lilli. Lilli and her Filipino husband, Allan, lived in the Bay Area and had three children. And Phil, with his second wife, Kristina, was in San Diego. They had three children by Phil's first wife, Gladys, and one stepdaughter. By 2003, I had seven grandchildren. At 19, Penni was the oldest. I was so proud of her because she had become a professional dancer and worked as part of Brittany Spears' group. I had even seen her on TV several times.

Lilli e-mailed me almost every day and, more and more, encouraged me to move out to California and be part of their lives. At first I passed this off, explaining that I lived most of my life on the East Coast and had grown deep roots. Besides, I was in my late 60's, and the enormous changes I would have to make might be more than I could handle.

But the more I thought, the more the idea seemed to make sense. And one night I realized something. When Lilli was 7 years old and Caroline barely old enough to even remember me, I left them and their two brothers by simply disappearing from their lives that day in the Philippines 33 years ago. Now, by asking me to move to California and be near them, they were giving me a second chance to be their father. I couldn't ignore this. It was justification enough to go, knowing I was lucky that they had even asked.

With mixed emotions, I resigned from Windstar in October of 2003. My friends threw a big farewell party with over 40 people showing up including Donnie and Nancy. A few days later, after the Sunday morning meeting, more friends gathered around my packed Ciera wishing me well. One of them gave me a packed lunch, which she had made earlier. It was a tearful goodbye.

I got in the car, drove out of the parking lot and headed up I-75, bound for California. Despite the fact I was 68 years old, I was embarking on yet another adventure.

CHAPTER 27

CALIFORNIA ODYSSEY

It took me five days to cross the country. Averaging about 600 miles a day, I had my first glimpse of the Rocky Mountains after I left El Paso, Texas, and headed up towards Phoenix, Arizona. The next day, passing through the town of Ehrenberg, I crossed over the Colorado River into California. The flat desert country seemed to stretch endlessly ahead, and the distant peaks of the Little San Bernardino Mountain range lay to the northwest. I had only 200 miles to go to Los Angeles where I planned to spend my final night. Then I would drive the final 500 miles up the San Joaquin Valley to the Bay Area where Lilli lived.

I was absorbed in thought as I watched the road ahead of me. Now that I was in California, it slowly began to dawn on me what a big change in my life I was attempting. I felt pangs of doubt for the first time. Was I doing the right thing? At 68 years old and set in my ways, I was leaving behind a crowd of friends and a lifetime on the East Coast to begin a new life in a strange place. All of a sudden, there seemed to be so many uncertainties.

How would my children receive me? The familiar guilt started to come back. I realized I was a bit apprehensive staying with Lilli until I found a job and a place of my own. What would it be like to live with four others? Would it work out to share a home with her, her third husband, Jason, and my two grandchildren Samantha and AJ?

My sons were within easy driving distance, too. How often would I see them? Ricky and Jill Ann lived in Sacramento. Phil and Kristina had settled outside of San Diego with Kristina's daughter Reilly and Phil's family, Chris, Jessica and Phil, Jr.

So where in the state would I end up? And could I adjust to the West Coast style of living?

For the first time, I thought that maybe I'd bitten off more than I could chew. All these uncertainties seemed to bear down on me. Then I remembered what the recovery program had taught me: a person could live only *one day at a time*. This thought calmed me down a little.

By late afternoon the high, snow-capped San Gabriel Mountains rose to my right, and I could see the distant buildings of Los Angeles. By nightfall I was comfortably settled in a Hollywood motel.

The next morning I drove north towards San Francisco, going through the rich farmland of the San Joaquin Valley and finally into Concord by early evening. As I pulled up into her driveway, Lilli rushed out and we hugged. My long cross-country trip was over. It was November of 2003, and another journey was about to begin.

But this new one would turn out to be one of the most difficult periods of my life.

It didn't start out that way, though. Those first months with Lilli worked out well. It was a time filled with strengthening family ties and getting to know my daughter, son-in-law and grandchildren.

Penni, Lilli's oldest daughter, had moved out and was not there. She was on tour as one of Brittany Spears' backup dancers. Ever since she was a child, she and her sister Samantha had shown unusual dancing talents. I'll never forget one evening, still in Florida, when I watched her on National TV. It was the opening game of the NFL football season in Washington, D.C., and Brittany Spears was performing for the half-time entertainment. There Penni was, dancing behind Brittany, with three others. I was so proud that, despite being in my apartment alone, I cheered out loud.

So I moved into Penni's empty room on the 2nd floor with my grandchildren, AJ and Samantha, across the hall. (Samantha, like her older sister, would start a successful career as a professional dancer a few years later.) And I was immediately drawn into what grandfathers love to do. Almost every morning I took 14-year-old AJ to school and picked him up in the afternoon. And, occasionally, I would give Samantha, who was 16, a ride to her school, as well.

That first Christmas, the entire family gathered at Ricky and Jill Ann's home in Sacramento. Caroline and Sam came out from New Jersey, and Phil and Christina drove up from San Diego. Perhaps the most traumatic moments for me were when I met Lana for the first time in 33 years. She had migrated from the Philippines earlier in the year and had settled in Antioch. Our meeting was civil but uncomfortable.

After Christmas I began looking for a job. I scoured the San Francisco waterfront. I had high hopes because the city was a mecca for boat captains. There were more than a dozen ferries making trips to Alcatraz, Sausalito and Tiburon. Unfortunately, I discovered all the companies, including the most popular Blue and Gold fleet and Red and White Fleet, only hired unionized employees. This forced me to join the union, only to be told later that I would be put on a list and have to wait an undetermined amount of time for a job. So I looked for non-union jobs in Oakland, Tiburon and Sausalito. But by April I still hadn't found one.

All this led to extreme frustration. And, despite the initial excitement of being reunited with my children, I found it difficult to adjust to my new California world. Everything was strange and different. Traffic rules, in some cases, were not the same as on the East Coast. Life moved at a quicker pace. People drove faster. There were no shingled homes and village greens, no small town atmosphere.

In addition, I had less success making friends. It took a long time for me to realize that the reason for this was that I wasn't opening up and letting them in. This was because I had not entirely believed my California move would work out and that I might have to return to Florida. And the finality of leaving everyone back east depressed me. So for the first year, I lived in a kind of suspended animation, and my ability to set any firm goals was practically nil. I was afraid to do anything that might lead to any sort of permanence.

In this frame of mind, I drove to San Diego to visit Phil and Kristina for a few days. They lived in a nice house in Poway, a town 20 miles north of the city.

While I was there, Phil suggested we drive up to Newport Beach, 80 miles up the coast, and look around. Newport Harbor was one of the largest pleasure boat harbors in the country, and he thought I would like it there.

And he was right. We saw a number of whale watching vessels as well as harbor tour boats docked along the waterfront of Balboa Peninsula in an area called the "Fun Zone." Having a moderate honky-tonk atmosphere, the Zone boasted a Ferris wheel, a bumper car establishment, gift shops and restaurants. A couple of outfits rented out jet skis as well as small sailboats, and a large high-speed catamaran made daily trips to the island of Catalina 25 miles away. Finally, there was the Balboa Ferry which transported cars and passengers the short distance to Balboa Island across the way.

I had been prepared to go job hunting while I was visiting Phil, having brought my license and resume with me. So the next day I returned alone in my Ciera to check out possibilities that the Fun Zone might offer. In the first hour I handed out at least a half dozen resumes to whoever was in the offices of the various whale watching and charter fishing companies. And then I noticed The Fun Zone Boat Company, which was advertising harbor tours. Located next to the Ferris wheel, its ticket office was a small structure which looked very much like the pilothouse of an old Mississippi paddle-wheeler. So I walked up to the open ticket window where there was a man waiting for customers. I remember the conversation well.

"I'm a licensed boat captain, and I'm looking for a job," I said, showing him my resume and license.

"Really?" The man smiled.

"Do you need a captain?" I asked, holding up my license.

"Well, not at the moment. But let me take a look at your resume." I handed it over to him. It contained 8 X 10 photographs of all the boats I had commanded, in Cape Cod and Maryland, neatly arranged in a loose-leafed album. The man studied it for a few moments, as he flipped the pages, and then looked at me.

"I can give you some work once a week, but that's all," he said.

"OK," I replied, willing to take anything I could get. I had been lucky. The man was obviously the owner or one of the owners of the boat company, and he introduced himself as Wilheim.

"Could you come back tomorrow, and we'll check you out on one of our boats?"

"Yes," I answered quickly, not caring that a roundtrip from Phil's was over 160 miles.

The next day I returned. The Fun Zone Company had three boats. One, their party boat, *Tiki*, had two decks and was 60 feet overall. The others were harbor tour boats and slightly smaller. Wilheim, who had met me at the ticket office, walked down to the dock with me and pointed to the *Queen*, one of the tour boats, which was tied up at the end. We both went aboard. He showed me the controls, started the engines and then sat back and watched. During the next 10 minutes, I made three landings. Wilheim seemed impressed and invited me back to the office where we talked. He reminded me that he could only give me minimum work and that, if I liked, he could call me in three weeks when business would pick up with the summer season. I agreed.

I had been back in Concord at Lilli's for three weeks when, sure enough, Wilheim called. He said he could promise me one day a week with more days later on when the summer peaked. I told him I would come down as soon as I found a place to stay in Newport Beach.

A couple of days later, having said goodbye to Lilli and making the 500-mile drive down to Newport Beach, I found a residential motel on Route 1, 6 miles from the Fun Zone. Having settled in, and despite the fact that I had at least some work, I fell into a depression. Perhaps, it was because I had left Lilli, Samantha and AJ and now was living in a strange town in a motel without knowing a soul. Perhaps, it was because I was 69 and homesick for the life I was accustomed to at home.

It was the second or third day after I arrived in Newport when things seemed to come apart. The changes in my life were too much and too many for me. I just didn't think I could handle it. I simply wanted to go home.

I called my old friend Oona in Florida and shared with her what was going on with me. We talked for a long while, and then she suggested that I hang in for another six months. After that, if I felt the same way, I should return to Florida. She emphasized that, although being near my children was important, there came a time when I had to think of myself, especially at my age.

After thinking about it for a couple of days, I decided to stick it out until Thanksgiving. At that time I would have been in California for a year.

CHAPTER 28

RESETTLEMENT

A MONTH AFTER I started with the Fun Zone Boat Company in May, I was running the boats full time. By Thanksgiving, I had become a regular captain for them, working five or six days a week. The job's biggest benefit was it allowed me to finally grow some roots in California, so much so that I decided to stay for good. My mindset changed from "if" my move from Florida would work out to "now" is the time to settle into my new surroundings.

Specifically, my job was running the two 45-minute harbor tours. One was up to the head of Newport Harbor to point out the celebrity homes, and the other was out its entrance into the Pacific to see the sea lions who gathered on the base of the sea buoy. Each tour was narrated live.

By far the most difficult part of the job was learning and perfecting these narrations. Thanks to my days with Hy-Line and the *Patience*, I was already familiar with doing them on the microphone. Unlike the recorded narrations in Annapolis on *Harbor Queen* where I had to exactly coordinate the boat's position with what was being pointed out, I was required to memorize a 40-minute presentation for each trip. With six trips a day, I was narrating for four long hours.

The first tour was scheduled for 11:00. The last was 7:00 p.m. in the summer and 4:00 or 5:00 p.m. in the winter. We could have as many as 70 passengers or as few as four, depending on the time and weather. The company owned four boats. There were the *Queen, Belle* and *Showboat*, which all did the harbor tours and carried an average of 70 passengers, and the 149-passenger *Tiki*, which boasted a bar, a large area for dancing on her lower deck and a partially open upper deck. The *Tiki* was used exclusively for charters. I ran the *Queen* more than any of the other boats.

During my first months with the Fun Zone, I temporarily lived in a rented room in Laguna Beach, which was 8 miles down the coast from Newport. Eventually, however, I moved to a more conveniently located studio apartment on Newport Boulevard just two and a half miles from work.

RESETTLEMENT

When I could I visited the kids as often as possible. Sometimes, I'd spend three days going up to Concord to stay with Lilli overnight, then to Ricky's in Sacramento for a second night and back down to Newport Beach on the third day. I easily drove 1000 miles making these visits. Phil's house in Poway was much nearer, allowing me to spend the day there and return at night. Naturally, I didn't see Caroline and Sam much because they were in New Jersey. But, occasionally, Caroline would visit California during Christmas and, later on, I would travel east a few times to see her.

In general my life in California was improving and resulted in my opening up even more to making new friends at work and in the recovery program. Another positive thing was a resurgence of my photography. This happened because of my frequent trips to Sedona, Arizona, where my old *Yankee* shipmate Peter Bloomer lived. If anything can entice a latent photographer to bring out his camera again, it's the beauty of the Red Rock country and the rugged mountains in the northern part of this state.

Essentially then, my tenure as a California resident was becoming more full, and I was settling down into my new life more comfortably.

In the year 2000 when I was still in Florida, Donnie and I hired a full-time, live-in nurse to take care of Mom in Nantucket. At 94, she was still active and even driving her car. But she was becoming forgetful and somewhat frail, and we felt she needed supervision. So at some expense we hired a capable nurse who moved in with her on North Liberty Street. At first our greatest worry was that Mom wouldn't get along with the nurse, or worse, refuse to admit she needed one. But, to our surprise, she agreed.

By 2004 during my first year with the Fun Zone, Mom had aged a little and was still active. But our personal relationship was no better. This was seen during a visit I made to Nantucket prior to my move to California. I can't remember what it was all about, but we got into a heated argument. Little did I know that this was to be the last time I would ever see Mom.

Three months after I started to work at the Fun Zone in late July, I got a call from Donnie. He told me Mom had fallen going downstairs and had broken her hip. She had been taken to the hospital. For the next two days, we traded calls back and forth as Donnie updated her situation.

During the afternoon of the third day, while I was running a harbor tour and narrating, my cell phone rang. Breaking off my talk, I answered and heard Donnie's voice say Mom had died. It was a moment I'll never forget. I had 60 paying passengers aboard, and I knew I had to continue the narration. It seemed like an eternity before I was docking the boat a half hour later. When the passengers disembarked and I stepped foot onto the dock, the realization hit me. She was gone.

Mixed feelings began to confuse me. I felt a surprising deep loss and sadness. But I also felt relieved. The constant pain of our tainted relationship was over. And the tension of the interminable financial worries over the past years would end. Now, Donnie and I would be inheriting a comfortable amount of money.

These converging feelings of loss and relief fought each other as I prepared to fly to Nantucket for her funeral. The fact that Lilli and granddaughter Samantha had decided to come to support me made things easier. On a cloudy morning, we buried Mom next to Dad in the cemetery near my old walkup apartment on New Lane.

After the funeral I returned to my small studio apartment on Newport Boulevard and began to make some changes. I realized that now I could afford a better place. I could buy a nice BMW or Mercedes or put a down payment on a nice house or take a cruise to the Caribbean. Instead, out of habit, perhaps, I chose to continue my modest life. I found a two-bedroom apartment in downtown Costa Mesa, kept my Toyota and resumed working. This apartment was located in a gated rental community called South Pointe. Then, at great expense, I hired an 18-wheel truck to transport all my furniture cross country from Naples.

South Pointe was to be my home for the next three and a half years. During that time I continued to feel more at home in California, and I started to build a solid network of friends. Now, in addition to the children and the job being the first real roots I had grown in my new apartment, this network became an important third root.

As I did in Florida, I became active in the program and went to meetings daily. It wasn't long before I was being asked to speak at some of them. It was at one of these meetings that I attended regularly where I met Logan, who would end up being one of my closest friends.

Logan and I had an interesting and unique connection. At one of my first meetings, I shared my experiences with Sterling Hayden in Tahiti and with my own schooner 46 years before in 1958. After the meeting, Logan came up to me and introduced himself. He asked exactly when I had been in Papeete. I told him, and it turned out that both of us had been there at the same time. The strange thing about this was that neither of us remembered meeting the other. This was odd because, in those days, the number of visiting Europeans and Americans in town was extremely small. Also, Papeete itself was a frontier town having just one four-floor hotel. And there were only three bars. Both being drinkers, the odds were more than good that we would have met. The only explanation for us not meeting was that we were usually drunk in these bars, and the booze had blurred our memories. From that moment on, Logan and I became close companions.

Aside from traveling around the state to see the children, I also took extended trips to the East Coast. During the holidays I went to Florida to stay with Donnie and Nancy. And as I've mentioned before, I visited my old shipmate Peter Bloomer in Arizona at least six times while I lived at South Pointe. I was allowed this time off from the job because Henk, Wilheim's brother, had taken over the company. He turned out to be a very generous employer.

RESETTLEMENT

So, as long as we gave him ample notice, he would let us take trips almost anytime we wanted.

It was ironic that I had to resettle 3000 miles away to start seeing Paul again. It had been 10 years since I had seen my best friend. Now, I was able to go to Connecticut every fall, sometimes in the spring, too, to participate in the hawk watches. Our reunions were always happy ones, and it was as if we had never been separated over the last decade. And I loved being back in New England, too.

I even made it back to Cape Cod. Because I had lived there for so long and had been active in the program, I had many friends who I hadn't seen for a long time. Among them were Katrina, Tom Jones and everyone I had worked with at Hy-Line. And then there was Jeff.

For years when I lived on the Cape, I would sit next to Jeff at the Thursday night meeting in Cotuit. We were always beside each other in the same seats. Now, after so long I looked forward to returning to that meeting during the one Thursday I'd be on the Cape. As I walked into the meeting room, sure enough, there was Jeff sitting in the same chair. And my old seat next to him was empty. We had an emotional hello, talked about old times and then sat down at the start of the meeting. I happened to glance at him, and I thought I saw tears in his eyes.

My trips to Naples to see Donnie and Nancy were always meaningful. I usually stayed a week. And my first visit, shortly after Mom died, was particularly special. Besides having quality time with my brother and sister-in-law, I saw my old recovery program friends and also Oona and Dick Tully, my Cape Cod buddies. One day I rented a car and drove all the way up to Sarasota to see Father Joe, who was now running a parish there.

I think the most significant thing that happened at this time was that Nancy and I saw each other for the first time since our divorce. She had bought a condo in Jupiter in the same building as Jill's. Taking advantage of this, I rented another car, drove across the state, and the three of us had dinner. Because I spent the night in Jill's condo, Nancy and I were able to have some time together alone. It turned out to be a warm reunion. I think we both realized that there was a part of each of us which still loved the other. From that time on, Nancy and I have enjoyed a very special friendship.

The only sad moment I had during this visit was when I learned that Jack Kern of Unity had died. Along with Katrina I have always considered him a spiritual mentor.

Every year after that initial trip to Naples, I visited my brother at least once. And upon each return to California, I felt a little of that discomfort and doubt that I had experienced back in my first year in California. But these emotions always left after I had been back a few days.

I turned 73 the summer of 2008. Increasingly, I had been having thoughts of moving into a senior community so that, if my health deteriorated, I would have available help and not be a burden to my children. So in October of that year, I reluctantly left my apartment at South Pointe and transferred to a one-bedroom apartment in Costa Neuporte, which was only two miles away. Located in one large three-story building, this community served meals in a dining room, had a beautiful lobby, offered nights of bingo and pool in rooms on the second floor and free maid service.

I didn't know that in the next two years I was to face the most difficult period of my elderly life.

CHAPTER 29

I'M DONE

For six months I enjoyed the amenities of Costa Neuporte. Every day two maids came to my third-floor apartment to make up my bed, vacuum and clean. They also changed my sheets once a week. The meals that were served in the big dining room downstairs were excellent. And if anything needed to be fixed in the apartment, like the plumbing or cable vision, a maintenance man would be up in an hour. These perks made for a high rent, but I could afford it.

Among the 100 or so residents, a few became friends, particularly the group at the dining room table where I sat regularly.

I was surprised to learn that I was the youngest resident there. Most were in their 80's and Dorothy, a spry, cheerful 98-year-old, was probably the oldest and, ironically, became one of my best friends. A few of the residents required assisted living, and it was not unusual to see nurses and nurses' aides around the building.

I liked it at Costa Neuporte, although sometimes it was depressing to see the frail elderly using walkers every day or to watch the same individuals sitting in the same lobby sofas staring into space.

It seemed I had almost everything I could want. I had a job I liked, good health, despite my past coronary problems, and 10 grandchildren scattered around the state that I could see anytime I wanted. And because of my involvement in the recovery program, I had lots of friends of all ages. The program also helped me to fulfill a dream I had always had. I was asked to be a speaker at the program's annual convention held at the Hilton Hotel in Costa Mesa. My life appeared full and rewarding.

Then, without warning, things changed drastically in 2008. I had invested most of my money in real estate and mortgage lending because these areas were very active and profitable. But, suddenly, the financial crash came and, in a blink of an eye, I found my funds reduced to practically nothing. Life did an about face on me. I was like the proverbial CEO who was forced to deliver pizza for a living.

It became almost impossible to pay my rent and bills. At the end of each month, my bank account was only a few dollars more than empty. I couldn't afford the trips to Arizona, Florida and Connecticut any longer. Suddenly, I had to worry about the price of gas for the first time. And I found myself collecting coupons, something I'd never done before. I saw that I was being forced to change my lifestyle.

For the next year, it was a struggle to keep my head above water. It was only because of Lilli, Ricky and Phil that I was able to hang on financially. They sent me monthly remittances which, added to my social security, helped me from going under. I struggled, living paycheck to paycheck, remittance to remittance. But it was becoming more and more obvious that I could not remain at Costa Neuporte much longer, finally, in 2009, I filed for bankruptcy.

Believe it or not, personal growth and positive things happened to me during this difficult period. By now I had been with the Fun Zone for six years. Being around the waterfront so much, I saw myself becoming one of its "characters." More and more I was referred to as "Captain Win." This occurred not only on the job but among my Costa Neuporte and program friends. And whenever I was scheduled to speak, this reference was used on the announcement flyers and convention schedule. This soothed my ego. And friends, seeing me struggle with my financial woes, came to my support. They reminded me to live life one day at a time. They suggested I not take myself too seriously. And, most importantly, they reminded me of the enormous benefits of being of service to others. In helping your fellows, someone remarked, you were helping yourself.

An interesting example of this was the story of 22-year-old Jessica. One night at a meeting, I listened as she described in tears how she had lost her job and couldn't pay the rent. Later, I asked if working on the water appealed to her and that I might possibly be able to find her some work. She nodded yes.

The next morning I called Henk at the office and asked him if he was interested in taking on another deckhand. A minute later I called Jessica and told her to get down to the Fun Zone right away because Henk wanted to interview her. One hour later she was in Henk's office and was offered a job.

But that was only the beginning. In the following months Jessica became my regular deckhand. This gave me the chance to teach her about boat handling, seamanship and simple navigation. She took to the job quickly and showed natural ability in handling the *Queen*, learning the narration and dealing with the passengers. We worked well as a team, too.

We also had a little fun. For instance, whenever a friend of ours took a trip with us, we'd surprise him or her. As we were passing any one of the dozens of million dollar homes on the water, whoever was doing the narration would announce to the passengers that it was owned by our friend. On another occasion I remember having a private charter of businessmen. There was a thick fog with no visibility, and I was at the wheel with Jessica standing beside me. Both of us were looking ahead intensely when one of the businessmen approached me from behind.

"How can you see? Do you know where we are, Captain?"

I turned to him and said, "I have absolutely no idea, sir." With his eyebrows raised and with Jessica stifling a laugh beside me, he took a swallow from his drink, shrugged his shoulders and walked away.

One morning when we were working together, she asked me whether it was difficult to get a captain's license. I explained that a lot of studying was involved and that one had to have a certain amount of sea time. She said she was determined to get one. And she did. After working at the Fun Zone for a year, she was able to accumulate the necessary time. Then she took the extensive examination and passed it. Jessica became a verified captain.

At the same time I decided to let my license expire. My reason was that in doing so, I would open up a potential captain's position to someone younger who needed the experience. My job, however, didn't change much. The only difference was that I had to have a licensed captain aboard. Other than that, I still ran the boat and continued doing the narration as a deckhand, yet, free of any responsibility. Now, the captain was in charge, not me.

One day, shortly after Jessica had gotten her license and I had let mine expire, I came to the office ready for a day's work. As I looked at the note board to see who I was scheduled with, I saw Jessica's name, an irony of ironies. Our roles had been reversed. She had been my deckhand for almost two years. Now I was hers.

The point of the story about Jessica is that, because I deliberately put myself in a position to help someone, I had helped myself. For the period of time it took her to get the job and eventually become captain, my role in her success allowed me to often forget the dramatic changes in my life and concentrate on helping someone else.

But my financial situation didn't go away. By the winter of 2010, it was obvious I could no longer afford to stay in Costa Neuporte. Consequently, I began looking for a less expensive apartment in another senior community. I found several. The problem was that each had a long list of people waiting for the next vacancy to open up. And some others wouldn't even consider me because of my bankruptcy status.

One day I was at a meeting in Villa Park, an area 20 miles to the north of Costa Neuporte. It was a group I had attended regularly and liked. There was a young couple, who I was particularly fond of, named Eric and Nicole. They lived in Villa Park and were in their 30's. That day at the meeting I shared about my efforts to find a cheaper place to live. After the meeting they approached me and asked if I was interested in renting a room in their home. I thanked them but said I was looking for an apartment.

Nevertheless, I thought about their offer for a few days. It had been the last thing on my mind. I had no desire to live with anyone else no matter how much I liked them. But I also had to admit that, perhaps, my pride was playing a big part in my shame of having to rent a room. After all, hadn't I graduated from

Groton, one of the most prestigious schools in the country, sailed my own schooner to the South Seas and been a published author and advertising vice president? With such a resume of success, was I to spend my last days renting a room? I could almost see Mom turning in her grave. To her I would be a resounding failure.

But the more I thought of Eric and Nicole's offer, the more tempted I was to take it. The rent they were asking was less than half of what I was paying at Costa Neuporte. I thought of how much that would relieve me of the financial stress I was struggling with. With what my children were giving me plus social security, I would be more than comfortable. Living with them would dramatically reduce the expenses of my monthly bills, allowing me a little elbow room to do what I wanted.

There was something else, too. Although Costa Neuporte was giving me all those amenities, living with the aged was often depressing. And what made me think that the other senior communities would be any different? But living with a young couple barely older than my oldest granddaughter would have the opposite effect. The atmosphere would be much more positive and keep me young at heart.

The following week I told Eric and Nicole I'd give it a try. On April 1st Eric and Nicole, plus four other mutual friends, helped me make the move to Villa Park. The only things I brought with me were my bed, TV, computer and bookcase. All my other furniture went in storage. This would be my 17th move since I was 21. I hoped it would be the last.

I had only been living with Eric and Nicole for a week before I realized I had struck a gold mine. It became clear very quickly that I wasn't just renting a room. With a total run of the house, plus two affectionate, tail-wagging black Labrador retrievers and our mutual program friends frequently dropping by, I became part of a family that no rent could buy. And, yet, I had my privacy, too, with my own bathroom and a comfortably sized bedroom with a computer and book corner. The grounds around the house were ample with a large backyard and a good sized porch looking out over the front lawn.

By the end of the summer, I felt as happy as I had ever been since my move to California, something I would have never guessed a year before. And through the winter into the spring of 2011, when I had been there a year, I was certain I had done the right thing. I loved living with Eric and Nicole and they loved having me. I became a close friend, and I also became a father figure. And to me, they were, in addition to my own children, a bonus son and daughter.

My health continued to be reasonably good, although at the age of 75, I had slowed down some and was thinking more and more about retiring from the Fun Zone. What with getting back into photography, by starting a modest greeting card business, and my continuing activity in the recovery program with 34 years of sobriety, I would still have a full life. My retirement would definitely not result in a life of watching TV and taking naps.

One Saturday at work, I realized that I had delivered over 9000 narrations in my seven years with the company. And I had to admit, I wasn't enjoying the job like I used to. Without planning it, I found myself in the small office standing in front of Henk's desk.

"I'm done, Henk," I said simply. With those words, I officially closed the door on what had been a spectacular seafaring career.

CHAPTER 30

A LOOK BACK

Since the day I walked out of the Fun Zone office for the last time, my life has continued to thrive. Retirement has not smothered my desire to dream, although the dreams aren't as grandiose as they used to be. I have smaller ones now which are more attainable and practical. My rebellious nature, which dislikes some things conventional, is alive and well, and the enthusiasm I have always had for life is still a part of me. And, occasionally, the salt in my veins brings me back to sea again.

Recently, I sailed on the 100-foot brigantine *Irving Johnson*, a model of the *Yankee*, owned by the Los Angeles Maritime

Institute. We were offshore off San Pedro, and I was at the wheel as we rushed through the water under full sail. I was feeling a twinge in my stomach as memories of the world cruise 54 years ago came back to me. Looking aloft at the foretopsail, I had the urge to climb up to my favorite spot, but I knew that my 76-year-old legs and weak heart would no longer get me there.

Not long ago I flew to Vermont to attend a reunion we called the "Birthday Bash." The entire side of Donnie's family, totaling 15 members, was there. Besides celebrating Donnie's 80th birthday, it was also recognition of my 76th and Brad's 52nd, Donnie's oldest son. It was a memorable and fun weekend enjoyed by all.

Both of these events - the sail on the *Irving Johnson* and this family reunion - have made me look back on my past more than usual. Sometimes it's almost like seeing a movie which, as a critic, I can review. It certainly wouldn't be a boring one.

I have gone around the world on a tall ship and then sailed my own schooner to the South Pacific. I have survived two failed marriages and am fortunate enough to be blessed with four children, twelve grandchildren and one great-grandchild. As a writer I have been a published author and written 11 articles for national magazines and 23 for regional publications. I have held 14 jobs in six different fields, including being an advertising executive, a limo driver, a boatyard rigger, an alcoholism counselor, a janitor and a shuttler for car rental companies. And on top of all this, I have had the opportunity of being a commercial boat captain for the last 18 years.

I realize there have been two principal things which have helped create this varied life. The first has been my enthusiasm for life, and the second, a determined free-spiritedness. And so I ask myself: What have I learned in the "classroom" of life?

One of the most important lessons, for me, was from Joseph Campbell, who urged us to "follow our bliss." To a great degree I have done this. There were times, of course, when I was forced to take on responsibilities and certain necessities were required that I was uncomfortable with or flat out didn't want. But most of my life, I have spent following my heart, even though it meant making some sacrifices and trade-offs. Because of this, I will never say to myself "I wish I had done that when I was younger," like so many retired people in their golden years. I managed to do these things and for that, I am grateful.

Another important thing I've learned has to do with priorities and what's important and what is not. For more than half of my life, I had the money to buy a home, a schooner, substantial land in the Philippines and almost anything else I wanted. I also attained the level of what the world calls "status" and "success." I became an associate creative director of a major advertising agency and, later, an author of a book. Society told me that attaining and experiencing these things would be the recipe for happiness.

Apparently, it wasn't. Because how am I now living so happily when the most significant thing I own is my Toyota Corolla car and my home is a rented room? The answer, it seems, is that true contentment only comes from within and the material and status things don't automatically promise serenity and fulfillment. Today, my wealth is in my friends, and my investments are in my service to others and my spiritual growth.

The third lesson I learned is from the recovery program - the value of acts of service for others. I shared the story of Jessica. But it doesn't always have to be something as dramatic as helping her get a job and a potential career, or helping an alcoholic decide to stop drinking and become sober. By doing little things, I help people, too. For instance, while I'm at the supermarket or post office, I have dozens of opportunities to make a person's day a little better by being helpful. As a matter of fact, every morning when I get up, I promise myself I'll try to make at least three people smile before bedtime.

A final life lesson I have learned is that I am unable to control life. I need help. It seems unrealistic to believe that I have been able to survive all the rough spots on my own, or that I planned the intricate events that have led to the remarkable experiences I have had. How could I have possibly planned the day I got sober 34 years ago? Or planned to have a great-grandchild? A Power Greater than myself must have been looking after me through the years. This realization of my powerlessness has been nurtured by the recovery program and by the odd trio of a Catholic priest, a Unity Church minister and a psychic. These three, Father Joe, Jack Kern and Katrina Gannon, have guided me on the spiritual path I now walk.

Do I have any regrets? Of course. There are two in particular. The first is that I wasn't there for my children as they grew up in Manila. I'm certain I would never have found the recovery program to treat my alcoholism had I stayed in the Philippines. I am not giving excuses here. But there is a very good possibility that I would have drunk myself to death, as happens to many active alcoholics. But I still think there might have been a better way to have left them - a way that could have made me a better father, despite the separation between us.

The other regret has to do with Mom. I can't change some of the feelings I have had towards her, or that she often treated me as a son who, in her eyes, was "less than." So often she made me feel that I hadn't matched up to what she thought I should be. But how sure was I that she felt so strongly about that? How much of my reaction was imaginary? Couldn't I have given her more slack? And I never really gave her credit for all of the things she did for me. She paid for my years at Groton and for college. She absorbed the cost of the world cruise even though she didn't want me to go. I regret that I wasn't more compassionate and understanding during our infected relationship. I wasn't aware that she was always doing the best she could and that she loved me in her own way. I'm not perfect, but neither was she.

Today, my spiritual growth is the most important part of my life. Religion has only played a small part in my spiritual growth. I heard once that religion is for people who are afraid of going to Hell, spirituality is for those who have already been there.

I feel a deep gratitude for the life I have lived. And, although I'm pushing 76, I'm ready for more of whatever is left of my life.

EPILOGUE

Although I finished writing this book at the age of 76, life has continued to provide me with interesting, challenging and sometimes formidable experiences.

After conferring with my sons and daughters, we all agreed that it was best for me to return to the East Coast and Naples where I could be at home near my brother and sister-in-law and my many old friends.

Packing my belongings into my 2005 Toyota Corolla, which had some 200,000 miles on it at the time, I embarked on yet another adventure of driving across the country. It turned out to be a 5-day trip which I thoroughly enjoyed. The reunion with my family and friends in Naples gave me a deep feeling that I had finally come home.

In the last 8 years, I have absorbed the gentle life of Naples and become more active than ever in the recovery program. Money problems have forced me to move a number of times from one rented room to another until I finally ended up in a comfortable apartment.

Recently age has caught up with me. It became increasingly difficult to live alone and take care of myself. COPD and heart problems eventually sentenced me to a walker. Six months ago I ended up in the hospital suffering from dehydration, congestive heart failure, and emphysema. I now reside in a nursing home where I have been forced to trade in my trusty Toyota Corolla for a wheelchair.

But thankfully, because of the program and my activity in it, life still has meaning and hope. I have loving friends who are willing to pick me up and take me to meetings around town, enabling me to continue my service to people by helping other alcoholics and addicts. Many times now I find myself saying to the newcomers at meetings "you see here an old 84-year-old man in a wheelchair, sucking on oxygen. But don't feel sorry for me because I'm still experiencing, after 43 years of sobriety, the joy of living that the program promises."

If I have any regrets, it's that I can't go out on the water anymore. But that's OK. Nothing can take away the memories of being at sea under sail, flying before the trade winds on the deep blue Pacific, listening to the tumbling bow wake and looking aloft at a cloud of billowing sails.

GLOSSARY

Abeam - off to the side of a vessel at right angles to the boat's centerline

Aft (after) - at, near or towards the stern (back) of the boat

Baggywrinkle - a soft covering for cables (or any other obstructions) that prevents sail chafing

Beetlecat - a manufacturer for a small sailboat originating in New Bedford

Bend - to lash a sail to the yard

Bow - the forward part of a boat, the pointy end

Fathometer - a depth finder that uses sound waves to determine the depth of water

Fisherman staysail - on a staysail schooner, a 4-sided sail set between the two masts above the main staysail, used in light to moderate airs

Footropes - each yard on a square-rigged sailing ship is equipped with a footrope for sailors to stand on while setting or stowing the sails

Fore (forward) - towards the bow (of the vessel)

Foremast - the mast of a ship nearest the bow

Foresail (fores'l) - a fore and aft sail set on the foremast or the lowest sail set on the foremast of a full-rigged ship or another vessel which is square-rigged

Forestaysail - triangular sail set on the forestay

Foretopmast - the mast nearest the bow of a ship

Foretopsail - a topsail set on a foremast on a ship

Foreyard - a yard on the lower mast of a square-rigged foremast of a ship used to support the foresail

Gaff-rigged mainsail - a sailing rig in which the sail is four-cornered

Gaskets - lines wrapped around a square sail

Halyard - lines attached to the head of a sail and used to hoist sails up the mast

Hove/Heave (to) - heading towards the wind, with a shortened sail, and with the wheel lashed, so the ship gives way and drifts in the direction of the wind

Lazarette - a small compartment below the deck in the aft end of a vessel, used for stores

Jibe(d) - turning the boat away from the wind so the stern passes through the wind and the sail(s) switches sides

Leech - the aft edge of the sail, connects the head and the clew (lower corner) of the sail

Mainstays'l (mainstaysail) - a sail set on the mainstay

Maintopsail - a topsail set on the maintopmast

Mast - The vertical spar (pole) that supports the sail

Parrels - a collar attached to the yard, allows the yard to slide up and down the mast

Port - the left side of the boat, or the tack a boat is on (If a boat is on "port tack" the wind is coming over the left side of the boat.)

Port-quarter - the rear left corner of a boat

Reach - sail with the wind over the side. i.e A Beam reach is the wind approx. 90 degrees from the bow, broad reach 130-170 degrees from the bow, or close reach with the wind 55-80 from the bow.

Schooner - a sailing ship with two or more masts, typically with the foremast smaller than the mainmast, and being gaff-rigged

Sheets - all lines on a boat which are used to control the in and out motion of the sail

Starboard - the right side of the boat (a boat is on a "starboard tack" when the wind is on its starboard side - coming over the right side of the boat)

Stern - aft (back) end of a boat

Stood in (stand on) - correcting course for a destination point

Topgallantmast - the section of a square-rigged sailing ship's mast immediately above the topmast

Tops'ls (topsails) - a sail set on a ship's topmast

Yard - a spar (pole) on a mast from which sails are set

Yardarm - the outer extremity of a ship's yard

Brigantine *Yankee*

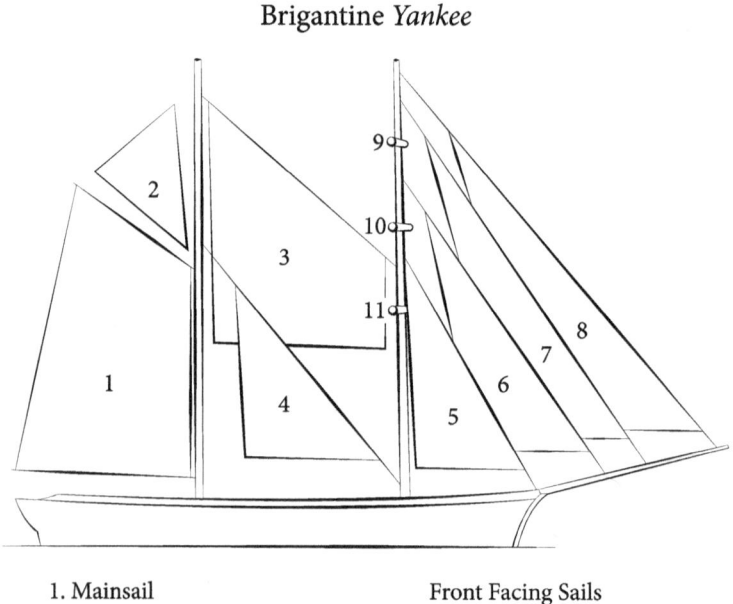

1. Mainsail
2. Main topsail
3. Fisherman staysail
4. Main staysail
5. Fore staysail
6. Inner jib
7. Outer jib
8. Jib topsail
9. Topgallant sail
10. Fore topsail
11. Foresail

Front Facing Sails

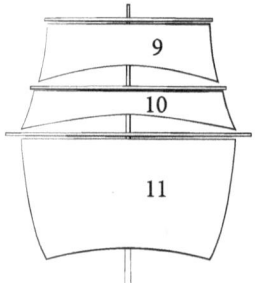

PHOTOBOOK

Elizabeth and Donald Williams - Win's parents

Mom and Dad

PHOTOBOOK

Bristol, RI, age 3 (1938)

Ready to race his Beetlecat boat (1950)

Playing hockey at Groton, age 16 (1951)

Scoring a goal at Groton (1953)

PHOTOBOOK

Riding a horse in Cap Haitian on the
second stop the *Yankee* made (1956)

Win, Mike Sumner, and Buzz Faucet on a
safari in East Africa near the Serengeti plane

The *Yankee*

Rigging on the *Yankee* (1956)

Irving and Exy Johnson, the owners of the *Yankee*

Age 21 on the *Yankee* (1957)

Ed Crosby and his Baggy Wrinkle Boys band

In Tahiti on the *Yankee* (1957)

PHOTOBOOK

Win's hut in Pirae Tahiti where his rent was $30/month

The back view of Win's hut with a sand floor

Sterling Hayden's boat the *Wanderer*

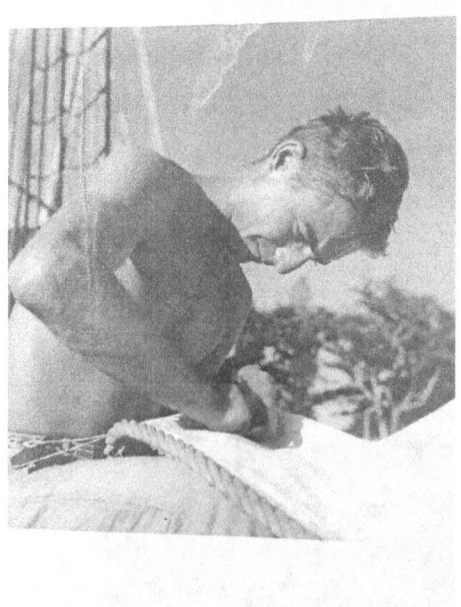

Sewing a patch on a sail on the schooner
Wanderer with Sterling Hayden (1959)

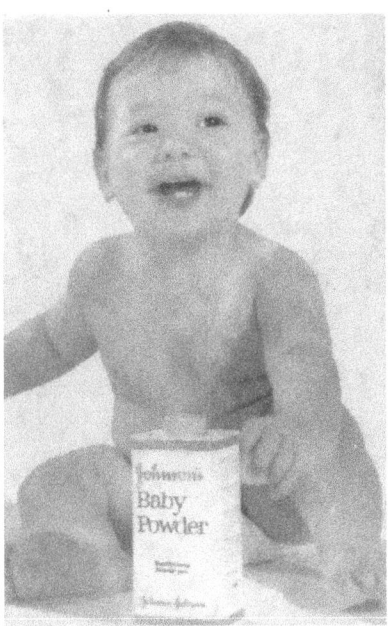

Philip, his son, the happy baby caressed with Johnson's baby powder, featured in Win's advertising campaign

Wins schooner, *Marie Celine* (1960)

Birding before getting sober (1975)

Marston Mills, Cape Cod (1980)

Brigantine *Romance* (1988)

On his last serious sailing trip on the
brigantine *Romance* in the Virgin Islands (1988)

Win's first command, *the Patience,* a tour boat (1993)

The Annapolitan II, Win's favorite command as a commercial captain (1998)

PHOTOBOOK

Age 64, Captain of *Harbor Queen*
Chesapeake Marine Tours (1999)

The *Annapolitan II*

Oxford Bellvue Ferry under Wins command (1999)

Win in California

Win with sister-in-law Nancy in Naples working for Winstar (2003)

Win with daughter Lilli, granddaughter Penny
and great-grandson Elijah (2008)

Lilly, Caroline, Philip, and Ricky- Win's children

Win and brother Donnie (2011)

PHOTOBOOK

Olivia, grandchild mentioned in the preface

Phil, Ricky, Win, Lilli, and Caroline

ACKNOWLEDGMENTS

I AM DEEPLY grateful to Lisa Groom, whose help and generosity made it possible for this book to be written. She spent countless hours of her own time preparing the original draft.

In addition, I want to thank Eric and Nicole Hoffman who helped me with the necessary computer technology which allowed me to end up with a presentable manuscript.

I am also grateful to all my friends—they know who they are—for giving me the encouragement and support to undertake this project and specifically to Merrill Noble, my niece, and Donald Williams, my brother, who provided me with the important family data that was needed.

And finally, I'd like to express my deep thanks to my publisher April O'Leary with O'Leary Publishing. Our meeting one another was a unique and unexpected happening which ultimately led to the publication of this book. To April I will be forever indebted.

ABOUT THE AUTHOR

Born in New York City in 1935, Winston Williams grew up in Mendham, New Jersey. He later graduated from the Groton School, Groton, Massachusetts and attended Trinity College in Hartford, Connecticut. The following years of his younger life were highlighted by a year and a half voyage around the world aboard the brigantine *Yankee*, sailing with the movie actor Sterling Hayden aboard the schooner *Wanderer* in the Society Islands, and taking his own schooner *Marie Celine* from Los Angeles to Tahiti.

Win eventually married a Filipina in 1960 and settled in The Philippines where he had four children and worked as an advertising executive. It was during this time when he began to have problems with alcoholism which caused him to lose his job and his marriage. Returning to the States, he settled on Nantucket Island, Massachusetts where he finally entered a recovery program in 1976 and has remained sober. Since then, he had his first book, *Nantucket Then and Now*, published featuring his original photography, he wrote countless articles for national magazines, including *National Geographic*, and worked as a commercial boat captain. Now retired, Win is active helping others recover from the disease of alcoholism. Win currently resides in Naples, Florida.

www.ingramcontent.com/pod-product-compliance
Lightning Source LLC
Chambersburg PA
CBHW071148070526
44584CB00019B/2704